Rose Elliot is the bestselling author of several vegetarian cookery books, including *Simply Delicious*, *Not Just a Load of Old Lentils*, *Your Very Good Health*, *A Foreign Flavour*, *Gourmet Vegetarian Cooking* and *Rose Elliot's Vegetarian Mother and Baby Book* (all available in Fontana). Born in 1945, she lives in Hampshire with her husband Anthony and three daughters, Katy, Margaret and Claire.

A vegetarian since the age of three, she has never eaten meat, but loves the scope which vegetarian cookery gives for imagination and creativity. She contributes regularly to the leading vegetarian magazine, the *Vegetarian*, presents frequent cookery demonstrations, and broadcasts on radio and television.

Rose Elliot has recently been developing her other great interest, astrology. She writes a regular astrological page in *Here's Health* and *Woman's Realm* and, with her husband, uses a computer to provide personal astrological advice, including character analyses and yearly forecasts. (For more details, please send SAE to Rose Elliot, PO Box 16, Eastleigh SO5 6BH.)

Rose Elliot

BEANFEAST

Fontana Paperbacks

First published by The White Eagle Publishing Trust 1975
This edition, completely revised and expanded,
first published in 1985 by Fontana Paperbacks
8 Grafton Street, London W1X 3LA
Second impression June 1986

Illustrations in this edition by Vana Haggerty

Set in Linotron Plantin
Made and printed in Great Britain by
William Collins Sons & Co. Ltd, Glasgow

Contents

Introduction

Wholefoods are for everyone. They're the grains, nuts and seeds, fruits and vegetables which have nurtured the race from time immemorial. They're our first food, our best food. It's a sad reflection on our time that to many people these most basic of foods are strange and unfamiliar. Their place in our larders has been taken by products which have been manufactured from them and now bear little or no resemblance to the original foods. Goodness has been taken out and replaced by 1800-plus flavourings, colourings, stabilizers, emulsifiers, bleaches, glazes, antioxidants and preservatives. Many of these are now being linked with increasing allergies and, dramatically in some cases, with hyperactivity, aggression and delinquency in children.

So I think it's high time to call a halt. To get back to basics. To bypass the pre-packaged rubbish. To rediscover the flavour of real food and the feeling of vitality and well-being which it brings. If you agree (and want to save money and make better use of the world's food resources too) come on in – and have a beanfeast.

Equipment

The right equipment makes all the difference to any cook but is especially important to the wholefood cook. I think the work involved in wholefood cookery is often overemphasized, but there's no doubt that a fair amount of chopping vegetables, grinding nuts and seeds and whizzing up pulses is involved. A food processor will make short work of all these tasks, save you hours of time over the year and enable you to produce wonderful dishes. If you haven't got one already and are thinking of changing over to wholefood eating, you'll be able to pay for it out of the money you'll save through serving pulse, grain and salad main meals instead of meat!

If you haven't a food processor, a strong liquidizer can be used for grinding nuts and making purées, and an electric grater for vegetables. A little electric coffee mill makes an excellent job of powdering small quantities of nuts and seeds.

Other essential equipment is a really sharp medium-sized knife (you won't regret the extra cost of investing in a Sabatier one), a good solid wooden chopping board and a 'box' grater which you can stand on the board to grate small quantities of fruits and vegetables and ingredients like orange rind. You'll need a large strong metal sieve for sifting flour and (lined with some muslin or gauze from the chemist) for making some of the recipes in the Home Industries section such as ghee (page 119) and soya milk (page 110).

I also include amongst my most useful time-saving equipment a number of casseroles which can be used on top of the stove (for preliminary cooking) and then go into the oven or under the grill, saving time and washing up. Pyrex make these, and there is the Le Creuset and Vision range.

Wholefood larder

Someone said to me the other day that she'd like to use more wholefoods but she felt lost when she went into a health shop and saw all the packets of strange ingredients that she didn't know how to use. Yet they're all so simple, really! And many are just as quick to use as 'convenience' foods, once you know how. So here's a guide.

Cereals and Cereal Products

WHOLE GRAINS   *Brown rice:* looks like a brown version of ordinary rice, and is lighter when cooked. Get long grain and cook according to directions on page 60. Takes longer than white rice to cook but tastes delicious. *Wholewheat, barley, rye and oat grains:* the brown grains, untreated. Useful for sprouting, see page 118. *Buckwheat:* not a true grain, but always classified as such; triangular in shape, dark brown if ready-roasted, light brown otherwise. Roasted has more flavour. Basic recipe for using on page 57. *Millet:* a small, round, golden grain. Cooks quickly, rich in protein. See recipe on page 58.

OTHER GRAINS *Wheat germ:* the vitamin- and mineral-rich heart of the wheat grain which is removed during the milling of white flour. A useful source of nourishment when sprinkled over breakfast cereals, salads and puddings. *Bulgur wheat:* looks like golden-brown wheat germ in the packet. Wheat which has been cracked and steamed. Can be soaked and used in salads or muesli or served hot, as on page 57. *Wheat, barley, rye and oat 'flakes':* whole grains which have been flattened into flakes with rollers. The oats are usually called 'jumbo'; *rolled oats* are a whole grain that you can buy almost anywhere. A mixture of these grains is nice in a muesli base, see page 22.

FLOURS *Rye, barley, brown rice and buckwheat flours* are all available and can be added in small quantities to vary homemade bread and add to pancake batters. *Brown rice flour* makes a useful milk pudding for babies (see *Rose Elliot's Vegetarian Mother and Baby Book*, Fontana). Most useful flour is, of course, *wholemeal flour*, sometimes called *wholewheat* (the two terms are interchangeable but not to be confused with wheatmeal). 100% wholewheat flour means it has been made from the whole wheat grain (described above); 85% wholewheat means 15 per cent of the grain (the coarsest bran) has been removed. 100% wholewheat flour is the healthiest choice and you can buy a bag of plain and add baking powder as necessary (to save buying self-raising as well). See Wholemeal Flour . . . Help! (pages 96–106) for more about this. *Arrowroot flour* isn't made from a grain but from a starchy tuber and is the wholefood alternative to cornflour, liked by nature-cure doctors for its soothing effect on the digestive system.

FLOUR PRODUCTS *Wholemeal bread:* it's good to see so much of it around now although the pre-packed loaves you can buy in supermarkets do contain additives. Best to buy from a reliable health shop or a baker who uses traditional methods (if you can find one). Or be sure what's in it by making your own: it's easy – see page 104. *Pasta:* wholewheat and buckwheat varieties both available and in an increasing number of different shapes. Looks dark in the pack but is much paler when cooked. I like the rings (anelli) best; they seem lightest.

Nuts and Seeds

Buy in small quantities from a shop with a quick turnover: rancid nuts are bad for you. But fresh ones are excellent, with concentrated sources of many nutrients including protein and iron. Especially useful are *cashew nuts*, *almonds (whole, blanched* and *flaked)*, *brazil nuts. Dried chestnuts* contain more starch and less oil than other nuts and make good savouries: see page 82. *Tiger nuts* (sometimes called *chufa nuts*) are obtainable from some health shops. They're a little brown rhizome and look as if they're waiting to be planted in the garden. But they make a wonderful milk: see page 111. *Sunflower seeds* – grey seeds, 5–10mm (¼–½ inch) long – are also useful, and delicious soaked in muesli (see page 22); also, small quantities of *sesame seeds* which are tiny and beigey coloured and *pumpkin seeds* which are the biggest ones, flat and a pretty green. Can be added to cooked cereal and vegetable savouries, eaten as a snack, sprouted or sprinkled into muesli. *Tahini* is a paste made from ground sesame seeds and has a wonderful nutty flavour; it can be used in both sweet and savoury mixtures. It will separate on storage, with oil on top: this is because (thankfully) it does not contain stabilizing additives. Simply stir the oil into the solid part before use. Many makes of *peanut butter* do contain additives: best to buy a pure one from the health shop, or make your own as described on page 115.

Pulses

Dried peas, beans and lentils. Many types now available. In this book I've used *chickpeas, continental lentils* (both the small whole brown ones and the larger ones, sometimes called *whole green lentils*), *split peas* and *split red lentils* which you can buy at any supermarket, *red kidney beans, black-eyed beans* (with a black spot on them) and, especially good for sprouting, little round green *mung beans* and small triangular dark red-brown *aduki beans. Soya beans* are used in this book for making milk (if you're keen!) and there's a quick version made from *soya flour*, which is a soft pale golden powder. You can buy very good *soya milk* in cartons from health shops and some supermarkets. *Tofu* is a curd made from soya beans: you can buy a soft type in vacuum packs from many health shops, and some sell a beautiful firm tofu which you can slice like cheese. *Gram flour* is a fine golden flour made from chickpeas. Some health shops stock it but at the time of writing it's not always easy to get. It's useful instead of an egg for binding nut roasts and burgers. For more detail on pulses see my books *The Bean Book* and *Rose Elliot's Book of Beans and Lentils*, both published by Fontana.

Fats

Whether to choose butter or polyunsaturated margarine and cooking oils is still a contentious issue. What just about all the experts do now agree on is the need to reduce all fats in the diet. In addition to the straightforward saturated versus polyunsaturated fats issue, there's another factor to be considered. When oils are heated (while being processed, in cooking or in the manufacture of margarine) the 'cis' fatty acids (which the body needs) are turned into 'trans' fatty acids, which the body can't use and doesn't want. What's more, the body has to use valuable 'cis' fatty acids to get rid of the 'trans' ones, thus depleting its supply. So you get the ridiculous situation of people eating too much fat, yet being short of the fatty acids they need. These essential fatty acids are found in cold-pressed oils, in green leaves and shoots, in fresh nuts and seeds and, perhaps best of all, in sprouted seeds. At the time of writing, I am following the advice which Dr Alec Forbes (Medical Director of the Bristol Cancer Help Centre) gives in his book, *The Bristol Diet* (Century). That is, to reduce fats overall as much as possible, with small quantities of pale *unsalted butter* on the table, *olive oil* or *ghee* for cooking (easy to make at home by melting unsalted butter – see page 119), real *cold-pressed oils* in salad dressings, and the occasional use of *coconut cream*, a hard white fat with a sweetish flavour.

Sweetenings

See remarks at the beginning of (Almost) Sugarless Puddings, page 84. Look for really dark raw sugar, sometimes called *muscovado*, with the name of the country of origin on the packet. When buying honey, look for *organic honey* from non-sugar-fed bees. It's more expensive, but the real thing. *Reduced-sugar jams*, and jams made from fruit and an apple juice concentrate, can be bought from health shops and are delicious. *Apple juice concentrate* itself is also available from health shops and can be used as a sweetener, or diluted with water (tastes just like normal apple juice) to make a healthy drink for children instead of those horrendous dye-, sugar- and preservative-laden squashes.

Dried Fruit

A useful source of natural sugar as well as B vitamins, iron and calcium. Most supermarket dried fruit is treated with sulphur (to preserve the colour) and petroleum oil (to prevent it from sticking together in the packet), but *cooking dates* are all right as long as you avoid those ridiculous 'sugar-rolled' ones. '*Sun-Maid*' *raisins* in the red tub or little packets are also naturally prepared and produced. *Unsulphured dried fruit* can be bought from health shops. The *dried apricots* and pale fruits look darker and less beautiful but taste wonderful. Most delicious (and health-giving) of all are the little whole *Hunza apricots*, but watch out for the stones.

Flavourings

The need to cut down on salt has been well publicized recently, although in fact experts in healthy eating have been saying this for many years – one nature-cure clinic recommending only one flat teaspoonful of salt per person each day, to include all 'hidden' salt. Too much salt is a major contributor to chronic high blood pressure and strokes. The nature-cure people would also tell you that salt causes 'waterlogging' of the cells of your body and tends to deprive your tissues of vital oxygen. It also encourages arthritis. One of the most practical and dramatic improvements anyone can make in their diet is to decrease their salt intake (including hidden salt present in nearly all processed foods) and increase their potassium intake by eating more fresh vegetables. It's surprising how you can get used to less salty food if you gradually cut down. Using freshly ground black pepper and herbs and spices helps, too. You can buy a high-potassium, low-sodium salt, which in theory sounds a good thing, but it's better really to get used to unsalted food. In the recipes in this book, I've suggested flavouring the dishes with salt and pepper because, I regret to say, I'm not at the point where I can do without salt in my cooking, but I'm trying to cut down, and I leave it to you to put in the salt or leave it out, according to your own taste.

Yeast extract is a useful flavouring and it is possible to buy a low-sodium one. I hope the manufacturers of Marmite will produce a low-sodium version. *Miso* is a flavouring made from fermented soya beans and has a pleasant, savoury flavour, though this, too, is rather salty. The same applies to *tamari*, which is naturally fermented soy sauce and has a delicious flavour, but that too is high in sodium. *Cider* or *wine vinegars* are useful for dressings.

Carob powder or *flour*, a brown powder made from the carob bean, looks and tastes rather like cocoa, but is sweeter. It's rich in B vitamins and, like cocoa, it contains iron and other minerals, but unlike cocoa it doesn't contain caffeine, so it's better for you. I use it quite a lot in sweet recipes.

Fresh Fruit and Vegetables

It's encouraging to see more organically produced fruit and vegetables available in big supermarkets. Let's hope this trend will continue. When you're less sure of the origins of your fruit and vegetables, it's important to wash them really thoroughly to get rid (as far as possible) of any lingering sprays. Scrub apples if you're planning to eat the skin (and it's a pity not to), also oranges and lemons before grating the rind. Wash delicate fruit as thoroughly as possible, drain in a colander or on kitchen paper.

Dairy Produce

Most natural health experts advise a low intake of dairy products. It's worth cutting down on your milk consumption as much as you can and *goat's milk* or *soya milk* are generally considered to be healthier than cow's. Cow's milk should preferably be skimmed. Have you tried fresh *skim milk* lately? It's much better than the earlier heat-treated variety. Even the reduced-fat hard cheeses are high in fat, so use all of them sparingly: *Parmesan* is useful here because you can get plenty of flavour from a small quantity of cheese. Many commercial cottage cheeses now contain preservatives: read the label.

Quark is a smooth white low-fat cheese from Germany and is a useful product to use instead of cream. *Natural yoghurt* is still rated a healthy ingredient – but this does not apply to most of the natural yoghurts on sale in supermarkets. Make your own from a yoghurt starter or a spoonful of real live *goat's milk yoghurt* made by a reputable producer: your health shop is probably the best bet for these. When buying eggs, support 'chickens' lib' and seek out real *free-range eggs* – from some supermarkets now, some health shops or, best of all, from the farm gate. Eggs, like all dairy products, should be used sparingly, but when you do use one, it's nice to know it's come from a happy hen.

More protein for less money

As well as being an abundant source of natural vitamins and minerals, many wholefoods are also rich in protein. So they're particularly useful at the present time when many protein foods are both expensive and causing concern because of the saturated fat which they contain. Swapping some meat meals for ones based on grains, pulses, nuts and seeds will have a beneficial effect both on your health and your purse. And there's another point. You need to feed an animal with up to twenty pounds of cereal in order to produce just one pound of meat. One pound of meat would possibly serve four people. Twenty pounds of rice or bulgur wheat would make a pilaff to feed eighty! If we in the West ate more grain/pulse/seed protein ourselves, instead of feeding it to our animals and then eating them, there would be more food available for the starving people in the world.

But, you might wonder, are these vegetable proteins as good for you as animal protein? All protein is made up of building-blocks called amino acids. These are built up in different ways to make the various types of protein. Thus egg protein, for instance, has one 'shape', beef protein another, wheat protein yet another, and so on. There are twenty-two of these amino acids, and eight of them are called 'essential' because the body can't make them. And in order to be useful, these eight have to be present in the right proportions. The protein in egg is one of the most perfectly balanced from this point of view, but all the others, including meat protein, have a bit too much of one amino acid, a bit too little of another, to be completely usable by the body. The excesses just get wasted because there isn't enough of the amino acid they need to be matched up with.

This is especially true when it comes to grains, pulses, nuts and seeds. They are a little unbalanced from the body's point of view in that they contain a bit too much of one amino acid, a bit too little of another. This extra can't be used, so normally gets wasted. (This does not mean that if you're a vegetarian you go short of protein, though, because unless you're on a very, very meagre diet there's enough usable protein to more than meet your needs.) But where nature has been so marvellous is that the amino-acid patterns of the different types of vegetable and dairy protein (pulses, cereals, nuts and seeds, and milk) interlock. Where one has a shortfall, another has an excess. So by eating two (or more) types at the same meal you can marry them up thriftily and get the benefit of extra protein. Thus, though, say, baked beans and wholewheat toast are both useful sources of protein on their own, when you eat them together the sum of the whole is more than that of the two foods separately. It's the same with rice and lentils, lentils and nuts, rolled oats and sunflower seeds. It's satisfying to be able to plan dishes which marry up all the protein in a tidy way, and is a useful trick to know if you're managing on very little food. I've drawn attention in the appropriate recipes to this complementary effect at work, just as a matter of interest and to remind you of the extra value you're getting!

Bright breakfasts

Breakfast, according to nutritionists, is the serious meal of the day that most of us seem unable to take seriously. Not at that hour of the morning, anyway. But take heart! A wholefood breakfast can help, because it's really easy. You simply put out all the whole cereal foods in jars, together with a large bowl of fruit and some natural yoghurt, and everyone can help themselves to their own particular favourites. You might have: oat flakes, bran,* wheat germ, flaked wholewheat (from health

---

*If you're all right inside you will get enough roughage from a normal health food diet – that is, one that includes plenty of fresh fruit and vegetables, wholewheat bread, whole rice, etc. But if you've got any tendency to diverticulitis or allied troubles, a helping of bran each breakfast time can be beneficial (provided your doctor is in agreement, of course).

shops), milled or whole nuts or both, sunflower seeds, sesame seeds, pumpkin seeds (good for the male members of the family as it helps avoid prostate problems); washed raisins and sultanas, dried brewer's yeast (if anyone likes that sprinkled over their cereal, it's very nutritious – full of B vitamins – but has a strong flavour which I don't like). Alternatively, if you know everyone's tastes (and, biggest miracle of all, they actually coincide), you can give them muesli (see recipe below), which I think is one of the nicest health breakfasts of all. It was invented around the turn of the century by Dr Bircher-Benner, because he wanted to encourage the patients in his nature-cure clinic in Switzerland to eat more fresh fruit. He believed that fresh fruit and raw vegetables should make up the bulk of a healthy diet and maintained that a fresh fruit dish, muesli, followed by wholewheat bread, or toast, and butter was more sustaining than a traditional British fry-up because in the latter there is a bonfire effect – a quick burst of energy followed by that mid-morning feeling. With the fruit and wholewheat breakfast, the energy is drawn from the food slowly, keeping the energy level up all morning. It's interesting that modern opinion now tends to support this theory. Anyway, try it and see what you think.

Dr Bircher-Benner's muesli is different from most of the packet mueslis on the market, some of which would surely make him turn in his grave. After all, the whole point of his muesli was the fresh fruit, which all too easily gets forgotten with muesli mixes. Personally, I love the real fruit version, but my husband likes the chewy, more-apparently-substantial dry cereal mix (he does have some fruit with it too). So I've given recipes for both real Bircher muesli and basic dry muesli mix (which you can make up in quantity, for several days at a time).

If you don't like muesli, then there's fresh fruit, plain or with chopped nuts, raisins, wheat germ or yoghurt, the recipe for which is on page 109; dried fruit compote on page 92; or porridge, which is the healthiest hot breakfast. Raisins or sultanas are nice soaked overnight in water or fruit juice and served with chopped nuts, a sprinkling of desiccated coconut or some yoghurt; and Jordan's Crunchy (from health shops) is popular with the children, served with milk or soya milk or sprinkled over some natural yoghurt or sliced banana or both.

To follow any of these (or instead of, if you like a light breakfast), there's wholewheat toast or bread with (a very little!) butter and some honey, reduced-sugar or raw sugar marmalade (from health shops) or sugarless apricot conserve (page 116), or low-sodium yeast extract if you like a savoury taste. And to drink? Well, ideally, you should wean yourself off coffee and tea, although I know that's difficult. Some health experts say that one of the biggest improvements you can make to your diet is to give up coffee and tea. Fruit juice or herb teas (see below) are the healthy alternative; or weak tea (preferably China), or dandelion coffee, or one of the other coffee substitutes (which a lot of people like but I'm sorry to say I can't take to) from the health shop.

Real Bircher Muesli
Serves 1
Calories: 255–285

1 tablespoon rolled oats or 1 dessertspoon medium oatmeal
3 tablespoons water
3 tablespoons milk

1 teaspoon lemon juice
100–175g (4–7 oz) apple
honey
1 tablespoon grated nuts

Soak oats in water overnight. Next day, mix with other ingredients, grating the apple into the mixture and sprinkling nuts on top. According to Dr Bircher-Benner, the whole apple should be grated into the mixture, skin, pips and all.

The original version was made with sweetened condensed milk instead of the milk and honey alternative given. Ordinary milk was not considered safe at the time Bircher-Benner invented this dish. If you want to use condensed milk, use 1 tablespoon with 2–3 tablespoons water and leave out the honey.

Basic Dry Muesli Mix

It's easy to make your own basic dry muesli from natural ingredients, and to your individual taste. The following quantities are for a bulk mixture that will do several days at a time. You can serve the mixture dry, adding milk at the table, or put a portion into a bowl and leave to soak overnight (see below).

Makes approx. 1.5kg (3 lb 3 oz)
Calories: 100 per 25g (1 oz)

1kg (2 lb 3 oz) oat flakes
100g (4 oz) sunflower seeds
250g (8 oz) raisins, washed

75g (3 oz) chopped almonds or
   hazel nuts, toasted

Mix all ingredients together. Keep in an airtight jar or plastic container.

Alternatively, you can just make up a 'muesli base' using several kinds of rolled grain: a mixture of rolled oat (and/or 'jumbo oats' from health shops), rolled wheat and rye grains, called 'flakes' in health shops. To use this base, put about 25g (1 oz) into a bowl the night before, with 1 tablespoon sunflower seeds and 1 tablespoon raisins or sultanas and cover with cold water or real apple juice. Next day add fruit as required: chopped banana or peach are delicious, so are strawberries and raspberries when in season. It's very nice just like that, but can be topped with a spoonful of thick natural yoghurt, if you like it, or some milk or soya milk. Soaking the mixture the night before not only softens the grains making a delightfully creamy mixture, but also 'wakes up' the sunflower seeds and activates valuable enzymes to put a spring into your step! On the same principle, you can soak other grains instead of the oats, for a change. Try bulgur wheat, couscous and flaked millet. They're nice with sunflower seeds, as above, and raisins to add sweetness.

Porridge
Serves 2–3
Calories: 130–200 per serving

900ml (1½ pints) water
125g (4 oz) rolled oats or a mixture of rolled oats, rye flakes or jumbo
  oats

Put the water into a saucepan and add the oats and other flakes
if using. Bring to the boil and simmer, stirring occasionally, for
4–5 minutes. Good with a little honey or raw barbados sugar.

Herb Teas
These can be made from your own fresh or dried herbs, or the
herb tea bags you can get from health shops which are
convenient to use and come in a wide range of varieties. You
can make herb tea in a pot, just like ordinary tea, using dried
or chopped fresh herbs. Experiment a little to see the quantity
which gives the right strength of 'brew' for you. Or make the
tea in a cup, like this:
Makes one cupful
Calories: 0, but allow 30 for a teaspoonful of honey, if using

1 teaspoon dried herbs –
  peppermint, sage or
  rosemary, for instance

1 cupful boiling water
a little honey to taste, optional
thin slice of lemon, optional

Put the herbs into a cup and pour in the boiling water. Cover
and leave to infuse for 4–5 minutes. Strain if you like. Add a
little honey and serve with a slice of lemon.

Lazy soups

In order to qualify for this chapter, the soups had to be quick and easy enough to compete with tinned and packet varieties, like the first three; capable of becoming a complete meal-in-a-bowl like the quick onion soup and the continental lentil; or, like the dhal (not difficult if you have the spices to hand), too delicious to leave out.

Vegetable Stock

If you've got time to make some real vegetable stock, that will be a delicious addition to your soups, as well as adding extra nourishment. So will the water that vegetables have been cooked in: save this, with all its valuable nutrients, and store in a jug in the fridge.

To make vegetable stock, all you do is put a chopped onion, a roughly sliced bulb of garlic, 2 or 3 chopped carrots, a couple of celery sticks, perhaps a few outer leaves of lettuce or cabbage or the well-washed green part of leeks, into a large saucepan, cover with plenty of water, simmer for 30 minutes, then strain and discard vegetables.

If you haven't any stock or vegetable water, though, don't let this put you off making soup. You can buy some good vegetable stock cubes at health shops, and you can also make a delicious soup using ordinary water!

Quick Potato Soup
Serves 4
Calories: 80

1 onion, peeled and chopped
1 large potato, peeled and
  chopped
2 teaspoons ghee

1 litre (1¾ pints) water
sea salt
chives and parsley, chopped

Soften the onion and potato in the ghee in a large pan; add the water and simmer for 10 minutes until vegetables are tender. Liquidize; season. Add chives and parsley. Delicious with warm wholewheat rolls.

Quick Tomato Soup
Serves 4
Calories: 50

1 onion, peeled and chopped
2 sticks celery, chopped
2 teaspoons ghee
250g (8 oz) fresh tomatoes,
  skinned

1 litre (1¾ pints) water
dash of sugar
sea salt

Soften the onion and celery in the ghee; add tomatoes and water. Simmer until vegetables are tender. Liquidize; season with a dash of sugar and some sea salt.

Quick Onion Soup
Serves 4
Calories: 60

4 onions, peeled and sliced
2 teaspoons ghee
1 teaspoon caraway seeds,
    optional

1 tablespoon flour
1 litre (1¾ pints) water
squeeze of lemon juice
sea salt

Soften the onions in the ghee with the caraway seeds if you like them; stir in the flour, add the water and simmer for 10 minutes until onions are tender and flour cooked. Add lemon juice and seasoning. Serve as it is or, for a complete meal-in-a-bowl, in the traditional French manner: pour soup over toasted French bread in a piping hot bowl, top with a little grated cheese and, if you like, make it golden and bubbly under a hot grill. Serve with a green salad.

Continental Green Lentil and Vegetable Soup
Serves 4
Calories: 140

125g (4 oz) continental green
    lentils
1 litre (1¾ pints) water
2 teaspoons ghee
1 onion, peeled and sliced

1 cup mixed vegetables: carrot,
    cabbage, celery, tomato
1 tablespoon wholewheat flour
1 teaspoon yeast extract

Soak lentils in the water for half an hour or so, or overnight. Heat ghee in a pan, add onion and other vegetables and fry for

5 minutes. Add flour, lentils and their liquid, and yeast extract. Simmer until vegetables and lentils are tender – about half an hour. Season and serve with a little grated cheese or crusty bread to make it a meal in itself. This soup is particularly attractive served in chunky earthenware bowls.

Dhal Soup
Serves 4
Calories: 125

125g (4 oz) split peas
1 litre (1¾ pints) water
1 bay leaf
2 onions, peeled and sliced
½ teaspoon ground ginger
½ teaspoon turmeric

2 garlic cloves, crushed
2 teaspoons ghee
2 teaspoons garam masala
dash of lemon juice
lemon rings to garnish

Soak split peas in the water for an hour or so if possible, then simmer gently with bay leaf, half the onion, ginger and turmeric, until tender – about half an hour. Meanwhile fry garlic and the rest of the onion in the ghee until browned, add garam masala and pour into the lentils. Stir, and leave for at least 10 minutes for the flavours to blend – better if you can leave it longer. Season carefully and sharpen with a dash of lemon juice. Reheat, and serve with lemon rings in it.

   Eaten before a vegetable curry and rice meal this soup supplies additional protein which complements that in the rice.

Just a quick bite

Natural foods are inconvenient . . . take too long to prepare
. . . aren't suitable for the rush-and-hurry life most of us lead.
Well, maybe some of them aren't, but they're not the half of
it. What could be easier, for instance, than a handful of nuts
and raisins? Or an orange or banana and some yoghurt? Or a
bowl of muesli – why should it be just for breakfast? And what's
wrong with a wholemeal roll and cheese for a quick snack? Or
wholemeal pitta bread (which many supermarkets now sell)
filled with sliced tomato, chopped lettuce and cooked or
sprouted beans? Or, for the best snack of all, some homemade
hummus (page 75) which is a wonderful savoury purée of
chickpeas that you serve on a flat plate with a slice of lemon and
some olive oil and scoop up with pieces of warmed wholewheat
pitta bread or whole radishes, sprigs of cauliflower, sticks of
carrot and spring onions? Some of the bean pâté on page 81,

served in a small ramekin with fingers of crisp wholemeal toast, is also delicious.

Wholemeal bread makes an excellent basis for snacks, and sandwiches (made with lots of salad filling and little or no butter) are a real health food. So is wholemeal bread topped with one of the sugarless spreads in the Home Industries section or from the health shop, if you want something sweet. Here are some other sandwich ideas. The secret of making healthy sandwiches is 'think bread – think salad', and go very easy on the butter (or magarine) and the cheese.

SAVOURY

Slice of cold mushroom pâté (page 65) or pease pudding (page 73) with a mild wholegrain mustard (such as Meaux) or chutney (see the sugarless one on page 117);

A little grated cheese or vegan cheese with lots of salad;

Hummus (page 75) or bean pâté (page 81) used as a spread, again, with your choice of salad;

Tahini or homemade peanut butter (page 115) with shredded lettuce, grated carrot (sounds funny, tastes good), sliced cucumber, sliced onions or spring onions (if you're not feeling sociable), tomato, banana or apple slices, sprouted alfalfa or beansprouts;

Cooked beans lightly mashed, with shredded lettuce or cucumber;

Cottage or yoghurt cheese with salad or chopped fresh herbs – any of the salad suggestions given for peanut butter are also good here;

Avocado dressing, page 38, or sliced avocado, perhaps with lettuce or alfalfa sprouts or both, for a treat;

Low-sodium yeast extract (from health shops) with any of the salad suggestions given above under peanut butter.

SWEET

Clear honey mixed with finely grated nuts;

Cottage or yoghurt cheese (see page 108) with chopped banana, apple, dates or raisins;

Dates softened in a little boiling water then mixed with chopped or grated nuts;

The date spread or the sugarless apricot conserve, page 116;

Sliced banana, perhaps with a sprinkling of grated nuts or desiccated coconut, or with some tahini;

Tahini mixed with honey.

SNACKS

Mushrooms on Toast

Serves 2
Calories: 140 with one piece of toast, 210 with two

450g (1 lb) button mushrooms
15g (½ oz) butter
low-sodium yeast extract, if liked

2–4 large slices wholewheat toast
chopped parsley

Wipe – don't peel – the mushrooms; slice and fry lightly in the butter. Serve on unbuttered toast, sprinkled with chopped parsley. Toast can be spread with Marmite first if you like a more savoury taste.

Peanut Butter (or Tahini) and Tomato Toasts
Serves 2
Calories: 260 with one piece of toast, 330 with two

2 tablespoons homemade
peanut butter, page 115, or
tahini
2–4 large slices wholewheat
toast

3–4 large tomatoes, skinned
and sliced

Spread peanut butter on the toast, top with tomato slices and heat through under the grill.

Avocado Toasts
Serves 2
Calories: 320 with one piece of toast, 390 with two

1 large avocado pear
juice of ½ lemon
2–4 slices hot wholewheat
toast

freshly ground black pepper

Peel, stone and thinly slice (or mash) the avocado pear; sprinkle with lemon juice. Arrange slices on toast, or spread over toast, grind some black pepper on top, warm through under the grill.

Baked Potatoes

One of the great convenience foods, a jacket-baked potato makes an excellent simple snack if you've got time to wait for it to bake! Serve it plain with a very little butter – or, even better, just freshly ground black pepper or some cottage or homemade yoghurt cheese, or a little grated cheese. As with sandwiches, the healthy idea is lots of salad and little or no butter or cheese! Try it with a filling of shredded lettuce and tomato; with some mashed avocado; or with tofu mashed with chopped chives or spring onions.

Serves 4

Calories: 200 for the potato, extra for the topping (55 for 7g/ 4 oz butter; 120 for 25g/1 oz grated hard cheese; 20 for chopped lettuce and tomato; 60 for 25g/1 oz spring onion)

4 medium-large potatoes,   topping as required: see above
  about 225g (8 oz) each

Preheat oven to 230°C (450°F), gas mark 8. Scrub potatoes, then prick several places to allow steam to escape, then place them in a baking tin and bake for 1–1½ hours, until the potatoes feel soft when squeezed lightly in the centre. Serve with the selected topping, or with any salad: they're particularly good with the cabbage salad on page 50.

A salad a day . . .

You can't be in on the health/wholefood scene for long before you realize that salads are things to be reckoned with. Not your lettuce leaf, tomato, cucumber and egg-drowned-in-salad-cream type salad, but vast hand-thrown bowls of grated cabbage, carrot, celery, green pepper, onion – great vitality mixtures that are going to do great things for you, if only you can manage to get through them. The trouble is, you seem to have to be in such ripping good health to be able to!

Which is an unfair exaggeration really, because I personally love salads, but I do recognize that if salads haven't hitherto been a regular part of your diet, they do take a bit of getting used to. Like a friend of mine who went into a health food restaurant, glanced at the menu, saw Large Raw Combinations in the salad section, and left hurriedly for fear of what might appear.

The health people say that one main meal a day should be a salad. Many nature-cure doctors go even further and say that healthy people should eat 50–75 per cent of their food raw, whereas anyone whose health is less than perfect could improve things greatly by going on a 90–100 per cent raw regime. Many amazing results have been achieved on such diets ranging from cures for catarrh and eczema to arthritis, diabetes, arteriosclerosis and premenstrual tension. And they are an important part of the 'gentle' treatment of cancer.

A high-raw diet isn't as difficult as it sounds, because the more raw food you eat, the more you want. You can base it on your own favourite foods, with a breakfast of fresh fruit or muesli with fruit added; snacks, if required, of nuts, sunflower seeds, and fresh or dried fruit, and two large and wonderful salads for lunch and the evening meal. The trick is to vary these salads as much as possible, to include nuts, seeds and sprouted beans and grains for protein, and to serve the salads with interesting dressings. For a really strict regime (which is worthwhile if you want to get really well) you should cut out meat, fish, milk and dairy produce entirely. This, according to the experience of naturopaths and experts in the 'gentle' cure of cancer, is because these put a strain on the body's cleansing processes and interfere with the body's natural ability to heal itself. Don't worry that you'll fade away; this diet will enable your body to heal itself and you'll get all the nutrients you need from the fresh fruit, vegetables, nuts and seeds.

Once you're in good health, you can be less strict, allowing yourself wholewheat bread (which is not included in the original 'high-raw' phase of the diet because it is cooked), and a cooked savoury (such as those in the Main Meals section on pages 53–83) for one main meal. This should ideally be served with a large side salad rather than cooked vegetables, while you should still eat a large salad for the other main meal of the day, and breakfast should still be a fruit or fruit-and-raw-cereal meal. Milk should be kept to the minimum, but natural yoghurt (preferably made from goat's milk) and soya milk or tiger nut milk (see Home Industries section) can be used.

If that sounds appalling, all I can say is that people who've tried it say they'd never go back to their old eating habits. They feel too good, too full of energy, of joy and vitality. And of course, this way of eating is ideal for anyone with a weight problem. Salads save fuel and I don't think they need take any longer to prepare than other meals; in fact, once you're in the way of them I think they save time.

There are recipes for easy dressings at the beginning of this chapter and the salads fall into two categories: the complete-meal protein salads; and side salads, to have with a cooked meal instead of cooked vegetables, or for serving as refreshing starters. And, talking of starters, it's worth mentioning that that eminent doctor, Bircher-Benner, maintained that having something fresh and raw at the beginning of a meal aids digestion and helps the body to utilize protein more efficiently so that less is needed. Eating something raw at the beginning of the meal also means you avoid something called 'digestive leucocytosis'. This means that whenever you eat cooked food, white corpuscles rush to your digestive system, just as they rush to the scene of any infection. But when you eat all raw food, or something raw before eating something cooked, this does not happen, thus avoiding strain in your immune system and keeping it ready for any real emergency.* Your body likes raw food!

---

*Confirmed by research carried out by Paul Kouchakoff at the Institute of Clinical Chemistry in Lausanne in the 1930s.

EASY DRESSINGS

Vinaigrette
Serves 4–6
Calories: 35 for a tablespoonful

2 tablespoons wine vinegar, cider vinegar or lemon juice
1 teaspoon mustard powder

6 tablespoons olive or sunflower oil
freshly ground black pepper

Put everything into a screwtop jar and shake together. Keep in the fridge and use as needed.

Yoghurt Dressing
Serves 4
Calories: 18 per serving

150ml (5 fl oz) natural yoghurt
1–2 tablespoons lemon juice

chopped fresh herbs
freshly ground black pepper

Just mix everything together.

Tofu Dressing
Serves 4
Calories: 50 per serving

150g (5 oz) tofu
2 tablespoons wine or cider vinegar
1 tablespoon cold-pressed olive oil

chopped fresh herbs
freshly ground black pepper

Put tofu into a bowl and break up with a fork, then beat in the remaining ingredients. Or whizz everything together in a blender or food processor.

Mayonnaise
Makes about 200ml (8 fl oz)
Calories: 140 for a tablespoonful

2 free-range egg yolks
½ teaspoon dry mustard
½ teaspoon raw sugar
2 tablespoons wine or cider
   vinegar

200ml (7 fl oz) cold-pressed
   sunflower oil
2 tablespoons boiling water

Put the egg yolks into a blender or food processor with the mustard, sugar and vinegar and whizz until well blended. Then, with the blender or food processor going, gradually pour in the oil, starting very slowly. You can speed up once an emulsion is formed and you hear the sound change to a glug-glug. Finally, add the boiling water which thins and lightens the mixture. This will keep, covered, in the fridge for a week.

Tahini Mayonnaise
Serves 2–4
Calories: 70 for a tablespoonful

1 heaped tablespoon tahini
2 tablespoons cold water
1 tablespoon lemon juice

1 garlic clove, crushed
   (optional)
salt and pepper

Put the tahini into a bowl and gradually beat in the water and lemon juice: the mixture will form an emulsion, like an ordinary egg-based mayonnaise. Add the garlic, if you're using this, and some seasoning to taste. Some chopped herbs are nice added to this, too. Use as ordinary mayonnaise.

Walnut and Almond Dressing
Serves 4
Calories: 105–155

25g (1 oz) walnuts
25g (1 oz) almonds – whole, flaked or blanched
50g (2 oz) carrot, roughly chopped
2 tablespoons cold-pressed olive oil
4 tablespoons water
1 tablespoon wine vinegar
1 teaspoon chopped fresh rosemary, thyme or marjoram if available
salt and freshly ground black pepper

Put all the ingredients into the blender or food processor and whizz to a cream. Delicious poured over green salad or with hot wholewheat pasta.

Avocado Dressing
Serves 4–6
Calories: 105–155

1 large ripe avocado
juice of ½ lemon
1 tablespoon wine or cider vinegar
1 tablespoon cold-pressed olive oil
salt and freshly ground black pepper

Halve, stone and skin the avocado. Put flesh into blender or food processor with the rest of the ingredients. Whizz to a luscious pale green cream. Flavour can be perked up with a drop or two of tabasco sauce (go carefully, it's hot!) or a pinch or two of curry powder.

STARTERS AND SIDE SALADS

Alfalfa Slaw
Serves 4
Calories: 100

450g (1 lb) grated cabbage
2 carrots, grated

1 cup alfalfa sprouts
vinaigrette

Mix together all the vegetables; add enough vinaigrette to moisten.

Cucumber, Radish and Yoghurt Salad
Serves 4
Calories: 35

1 large cucumber, peeled and
  sliced
1 bunch radishes, washed,
  trimmed and sliced
125ml (5 fl oz) natural
  yoghurt

1 tablespoon chopped fresh
  herbs, such as mint or
  coriander
salt and freshly ground black
  pepper

Mix all the ingredients together; serve at once. Looks pretty garnished with some radish roses, if you've got the time.

Green Salad
For this salad, which is such a useful standby, I like to make the dressing straight into the bowl.
Serves 4
Calories: 100–130

1 teaspoon mustard powder
freshly ground black pepper
1 tablespoon wine vinegar
2–3 tablespoons cold-pressed
  olive oil

2 tablespoons fresh herbs,
  chopped
1 lettuce, washed and dried

Make dressing straight into a bowl: put mustard and pepper into the bowl and add vinegar. Gradually stir in oil. Just before you're ready to serve, add herbs and lettuce and turn lettuce gently until completely coated with the dressing. You can turn this into a complete-meal salad by the addition of some sunflower or pumpkin seeds and/or some sliced ripe avocado. It's also delicious with the thick walnut and almond dressing, the yoghurt dressing or the tahini mayonnaise given above.

Fennel and Apple Salad

If you like the aniseed flavour of fennel, it makes a crisp, juicy salad.
Serves 2–4
Calories: 90–180

1 good-sized fennel bulb
2 large eating apples

lemon juice or vinaigrette
lettuce leaves to serve

Wash and slice fennel and apple; mix together with a little lemon (or vinaigrette if you like) and serve on crisp lettuce leaves.

Orange, Cucumber and Mint Salad

Serves 2–4
Calories: 30–60

2 large oranges
½ cucumber

chopped fresh mint

Remove peel and pith from oranges; slice flesh into rings. Slice cucumber. Arrange on dishes and sprinkle with chopped mint. Very refreshing.

Tomato Salad
Serves 2–4
Calories: 50–100

8 tomatoes, skinned if you like

chopped spring onion
vinaigrette

Slice tomatoes; arrange on small dishes. Top with a chopped spring onion and a little vinaigrette.

Carrot and Watercress Salad
Serves 2–4
Calories: 15–30

4 carrots
orange juice

bunch of watercress

Finely grate carrots; moisten with orange juice. Serve piled up, surrounded by watercress. A pretty combination of colours.

Carrot and Celery Salad
Serves 2–4
Calories: 50–100

½ large head celery
2 large carrots

juice of 1 orange
handful of raisins

Slice celery; grate carrot. Mix together, add orange juice and raisins. Before adding, raisins can be steeped for a few minutes in boiling water to plump them, if you like.

Celery, Tomato and Avocado Salad
Serves 2–4
Calories: 140–180

1 head celery
1 avocado pear
4 tomatoes

lemon juice
dash of olive oil

Wash and slice the tender part of the celery (make the rest into soup/casserole later); peel and cut up avocado and tomatoes, then mix everything together, with a squeeze of lemon juice and a dash of olive oil if you like.

Spinach and Mushroom Salad
This is much more delicious than it sounds; in fact it's one of my favourites.
Serves 4
Calories: 75

1 garlic clove, crushed
1 tablespoon cold-pressed olive oil
2 tablespoons wine or cider vinegar

freshly ground black pepper
450g (1 lb) tender spinach, washed and finely shredded
225g (8 oz) button mushrooms, washed and sliced

Put the garlic clove, oil and vinegar into a salad bowl, grind in some pepper and mix all together. Then put in the spinach and mushrooms and turn them thoroughly in the dressing.

Raw Beetroot Salad

Another unlikely-sounding favourite. I like this sometimes for
my lunch, on a base of crisp lettuce leaves.
Serves 2–4
Calories: 70–105

1–2 large raw beetroots,
   scrubbed or thinly peeled
1 large eating apple or 1 large
   mild onion (purple ones are
   specially good)

orange juice

Grate the beetroot fairly coarsely into a bowl. Then grate in the
apple, or peel and thinly slice the onion. Mix with the beetroot
and moisten with orange juice.

Swede Salad

Another one which makes a refreshing lunch on its own,
without any extras.
Serves 2–4
Calories: 100–200

1 medium-sized swede
2 tablespoons mayonnaise
4 tablespoons natural yoghurt

2–3 firm tomatoes, thinly
   sliced

Peel and coarsely grate the swede. Put into a bowl with the
mayonnaise and yoghurt and mix together. Spoon mixture on
to a plate and put the tomato slices all round the edge.

COMPLETE MEAL SALADS

Stuffed Pear Salad

If you're on a high-raw diet for health reasons, it's best to use the nut cheese variation for the stuffing, but remember that this cheese needs to ferment for 8–12 hours before use (see page 114).

Serves 4
Calories: 170 (340 if using nut cheese)

2 ripe dessert pears
lemon juice
lettuce leaves
225g (8 oz) cottage cheese,
   yoghurt cheese, mashed tofu
   or nut cheese

2 tablespoons sunflower seeds
black grapes, fresh cherries or
   strawberries to decorate

Halve and core pears; brush cut surfaces with lemon juice. Place on lettuce leaves. Pile chosen cheese into pears. Sprinkle with sunflower seeds. Decorate with black grapes, cherries or strawberries.

Pineapple and Creamy Cheese Salad

Again, use the nut cheese variation if you're following a strict cleansing diet.

Serves 4
Calories: 150 (335 with nut cheese)

4 slices fresh pineapple
lettuce leaves
350g (12 oz) cottage cheese,
   yoghurt cheese, tofu or the
   nut cheese on page 114

toasted flaked almonds
black grapes or strawberries to
   decorate

Skin and core pineapple slices and arrange on lettuce leaves; pile up with chosen cheese, sprinkle with nuts and decorate with black grapes or strawberries.

Celery, Yoghurt and Date Salad

Instead of the yoghurt you could use the nut dressing, page 38, or tofu dressing, page 36.

Serves 4

Calories: 150 without sunflower seeds (allow 100 for a tablespoon of sunflower seeds)

1 large head celery
200ml (8 fl oz) natural
   yoghurt

175g (6 oz) cooking dates,
   sliced
sunflower seeds

Discard any tough celery stalks; slice the rest fairly finely, then mix with yoghurt and dates. You can add a few sunflower seeds to the mixture too, if you like. A quick crunchy salad.

Avocado Pâté Salad

Serves 4
Calories: 485

2 avocados
juice of 1 lemon
125g (4 oz) cashew nuts or
   blanched almonds
salt and freshly ground black
   pepper

drop of tabasco
lettuce, watercress, tomato
paprika

Halve, stone and peel the avocados. Put them into the blender or food processor with the lemon juice and nuts and whizz to a cream. Season with salt, black pepper and one or two drops of tabasco. Arrange on lettuce, decorate with watercress and tomato, dust with paprika. Alternatively, fill scooped-out tomato halves with the mixture if you've got time. It's also nice with a finger salad of radishes, spring onions, carrot sticks, pieces of celery and cauliflower florets.

Fruit Salad with Creamy Dressing

A luscious salad: a main course and pudding in one!
Serves 4
Calories: 480

2 apples, 2 pears, 1 orange,
  1 banana
a few grapes
a few lettuce leaves
225g (8 oz) cashew nuts or
  blanched almonds

300ml (½ pint) water
a dash of honey
a few chopped nuts

Prepare and slice fruits. Divide them between four lettuce-lined plates. Put nuts and water into blender or food processor with a little honey and whizz to a cream. Pour this over the fruits. Sprinkle with nuts – toasted flaked almonds are especially good.

Alternatively, make the tahini mayonnaise on page 37, omitting the garlic and herbs, and adding a dessertspoon of honey and (if you have it) a tablespoon of orange flower water and use that instead of the nut dressing. In this case, sprinkle with sesame seeds.

Aubergine Salad

This one doesn't really qualify as 'raw' since the aubergine is cooked; but it makes a nice change, perhaps served with a finger salad like the one described above.

Serves 4
Calories: 50

450g (1 lb) aubergines
1 garlic clove, crushed
200ml (8 fl oz) natural
  yoghurt

lettuce leaves
1 tablespoon chopped parsley
paprika
lemon slices

Wipe aubergines and bake whole on a dry baking sheet in a moderate oven until tender when pierced with a skewer. Cool, then chop and mix with garlic and yoghurt. Chill mixture and serve on lettuce leaves; sprinkle with chopped parsley and paprika and garnish with lemon slices.

Hummus Salad

Again, the hummus part of this salad is cooked, so serve it with lots of lovely crunchy raw vegetables to dip into it.
Serves 4
Calories: 300 a serving without extras; allow 125 for a tablespoonful of olive oil and 50 calories for vegetables

1 quantity hummus, see page
  75
paprika
cold-pressed olive oil
lemon slices

raw vegetables: radishes, spring onions, carrot sticks, pieces of celery and cauliflower florets

The recipe for hummus is given in the Two-Out-of-One section. (It saves time and money to make it out of a double batch of chickpeas.) Divide the hummus between four flat plates, smooth out so that hummus is about 1cm (½ inch) deep and covers the plate. Sprinkle with paprika pepper, drip a little olive oil on top and garnish with lemon slices. Serve with a big bowl or basket of the fresh raw vegetables for people to dip into the hummus and eat with their fingers. A favourite salad in our house!

Red Bean Salad
Serves 4–6
Calories: 165–250

1 quantity of red bean salad
  mix, see page 78
lettuce leaves

watercress, sliced tomatoes,
  beansprouts, radishes

Like hummus, red bean salad is in the Two-Out-of-One
section, and is made from a double batch of beans. It should
be served with lots of fresh salad if you want to count it as a
'raw' meal. Divide the salad between individual lettuce-lined
dishes, surround with watercress, sliced tomatoes, beansprouts
if you have any, and radishes.

Lettuce and Cucumber Salad
Serves 4
Calories: 56

1 cucumber
sea salt
1 lettuce
200ml (8 fl oz) natural
  yoghurt

chopped mint
2 carrots, grated

Peel and thinly slice cucumber, salt lightly and, if you have
time, leave in a colander with a weight on top for half an hour,
to remove excess moisture; then mix with yoghurt and mint and
serve on crisp lettuce leaves, surrounded with grated carrot.

Vitamin Salad

Serves 4
Calories: 245 (this allows for 1 tablespoonful vinaigrette per
  serving)

lettuce leaves
4 tablespoons grated brazil
  nuts
4 tablespoons chopped dates
2 tomatoes, sliced
2 carrots, grated

2 raw beetroots, grated
about 350g (12 oz) grated
  cabbage
½ cucumber, sliced
vinaigrette

Line plates with lettuce leaves. Mix brazil nuts and dates and
put in a pile in the centre of each plate. Arrange piles of the
other vegetables around this to make an attractive pattern – it's
very colourful. Pour a little vinaigrette over all the vegetables
just before serving so that they're all shiny and appetizing.

Rice and Avocado Salad

Serves 6
Calories: 390

225g (8 oz) brown rice
1 garlic clove, crushed
vinaigrette
2 avocados, peeled and sliced
2 heaped tablespoons sunflower
  seeds

6 tomatoes, skinned and
  sliced
sea salt, sugar
chopped parsley

Cook brown rice as described on page 60 (an extra batch cooked
when you're making a savoury always comes in handy). Mix
garlic with rice, moisten with vinaigrette and leave to cool if it's
still hot; then stir in avocados which have first been tossed in
a little vinaigrette, sunflower seeds and tomatoes. Check

seasoning – add a touch of sea salt, a touch of sugar if necessary, and serve sprinkled with parsley. The sunflower seeds complement the rice protein.

Rice and Curry Mayonnaise
Serves 6
Calories: 400

225g (8 oz) brown rice
2 apples, sliced
2 bananas, peeled and sliced
lemon juice
2 heaped tablespoons raisins
2 tablespoons sunflower seeds

1 onion, grated
1 tablespoon oil
1 teaspoon curry powder
100ml (4 fl oz) mayonnaise
100ml (4 fl oz) natural
  yoghurt

Cook rice as on page 60; cool. Sprinkle apple and banana with lemon juice and add to rice. Steep raisins in a little boiling water for half an hour to plump; drain, and add to rice with sunflower seeds, mixing well. Fry onion in oil with curry powder for 10 minutes, then mix it with the mayonnaise and yoghurt and serve with the rice.

Cabbage and Nut Salad
Serves 4–6
Calories: 210–320

350g (12 oz) white cabbage
2 carrots
2 sticks of celery
1 small red pepper
2 tomatoes
1 tablespoon cold-pressed olive
  oil

2 tablespoons wine or cider
  vinegar
freshly ground black pepper
125g (4 oz) roasted peanuts,
  cashew nuts or blanched
  almonds
125g (4 oz) raisins

If you've got a food processor, simply cut all the vegetables into rough chunks (removing seeds from pepper), put into the food processor with the oil, vinegar and a grating of pepper and whizz in short bursts until everything is chopped. Then add the nuts and raisins. Without a food processor, chop or grate the cabbage, grate the carrots, chop the celery, pepper and tomatoes. Put into a bowl and mix in the oil, vinegar, some pepper and the nuts and raisins. Either way it makes a filling meal served as it is, or with warm wholewheat rolls or jacket potatoes.

Carrot, Apple and Sprouted Chickpea Salad
Serves 2–4
Calories: 45–90

juice of 1 orange
2 medium-sized carrots,
   coarsely grated

2 apples, diced
175–225g (6–8 oz) sprouted
   chickpeas (see page 118)

Mix everything together; serve immediately. Some chopped mint or other fresh herbs can be added, also a spoonful of natural yoghurt, if liked.

Vitality Salad
Serves 4
Calories: 350

1 tablespoon wine or cider
   vinegar
3 tablespoons cold-pressed
   olive oil
125g (4 oz) sprouted wheat
   grains (see page 118)
225g (8 oz) sprouted mung
   beans (see page 118)

2 carrots, coarsely grated
50g (2 oz) raisins
4 tomatoes, diced
2 sticks celery, sliced
10cm (4 inches) cucumber,
   diced
1 raw beetroot, grated

For the topping
3 tablespoons natural yoghurt mixed with 1 tablespoon mayonnaise

Put vinegar and oil into a bowl and mix together. Then add wheat, mung beans, carrots, raisins, tomatoes, celery and cucumber and mix together. Divide between deep individual bowls, top with grated beetroot and a spoonful of yoghurt and mayonnaise topping.

Banana, Carrot, Raisin and Nut Salad

If the children are reluctant about salads, why not make a salad of all their favourite ingredients, even if it sounds like a strange mixture? This salad is an example!

Serves 4
Calories: 320

2 large bananas, sliced
2 carrots, grated
125g (4 oz) raisins
125g (4 oz) roasted peanuts

orange juice
desiccated coconut
watercress

Put the bananas, carrots, raisins and nuts in a bowl. Moisten with orange juice. Serve sprinkled with desiccated coconut and bordered with watercress.

Fast and flavoursome main meals

One of the complaints people make about natural foods is that they take too long to cook – all that soaking, grinding and chopping. Well, I agree, they can, but they needn't. Not if you've got this book, anyway, because in order to qualify for a place in it all the recipes had to be really quick and easy to prepare. (And if they didn't come up to standard, out they went – I've got a file to prove it!)

This section consists of three types of recipe. There are the Top-of-the-Stove Dishes, the first few of which are of the quick late-home-family-hungry variety; the rest, along with the Oven Dishes, while quick in that they don't chain you to the stove all afternoon, may take an hour or so on the stove or in the oven. In fact some of them – the sunflower seed hotpot, easy pasta bake and lazy lentils, for instance – were specially planned to cook slowly (either in a pre-set oven, or in a low oven that you can switch on before you go out) so that your return is greeted by the pleasant savoury smell of a meal all ready. But if you forget and return home exhausted, there's always too-tired-to-cook rice, which is delicious.

The other recipes, which I call Two-Out-of-One, are also easy, but they save time in another way. There's one basic mixture which makes two different savoury dishes. By that I mean different enough for you to be able to get away with them without the family saying 'not that again' (unless they're very cookery minded – in which case, what are *you* doing slaving over the stove?). These Two-Out-of-Ones save not only time but also power, and the extra dish will sit quite happily in the fridge for a few days or in the deep freeze for up to two months.

As I explained in the Introduction, I use a flameproof casserole whenever possible. This means I can use the same cooking utensils throughout some of the recipes. You may not have flameproof casseroles, so I have left it to you to transfer from pans to dishes suitable for oven or grill, as appropriate in the recipes.

TOP-OF-THE-STOVE DISHES

Quick Protein Potato Cakes
Serves 4
Calories: 380

450g (1 lb) potatoes, scrubbed
1 onion, peeled (optional)
salt and freshly ground black
   pepper
2 eggs
2 rounded tablespoons
   wholewheat flour

2 rounded tablespoons skim
   milk powder
chopped parsley, mixed herbs,
   yeast extract, as required
ghee or olive oil to fry

Coarsely grate potatoes, and onion if using; add salt and pepper and mix in the eggs, flour and skim milk powder to make a batter. Season with chopped parsley, mixed herbs, or yeast extract if you want a savoury flavour. Fry tablespoonfuls of the mixture on both sides in hot, shallow oil until golden and crisp. Drain well on kitchen paper. Serve immediately with salad, or cooked vegetables, gravy (pages 67–8) and apple sauce; or with fried onions, tomatoes and mushrooms.

The skim milk supplies protein which combines with that in the potatoes (yes, surprising, isn't it?), making this a protein supper dish in its own right, but it can also be an accompaniment to another main dish.

Quick Pepper Savoury
Serves 4
Calories: 270 (230 if using yoghurt)

2 large onions, peeled
4 large red or green peppers, or a mixture
1 garlic clove, crushed
1 tablespoon ghee
450g (1 lb) tomatoes, skinned and chopped
2 tablespoons sunflower seeds

1 teaspoon cinnamon
salt
150ml (5 fl oz) soured cream or natural yoghurt
2 tablespoons skim milk powder
soft wholewheat breadcrumbs
a little butter

Slice the onions and peppers, discarding pepper seeds. Using a pan or flameproof casserole, fry onions, pepper and garlic in the fat until tender, then add the tomatoes and sunflower seeds. Season with cinnamon and a little salt. If necessary, turn into a dish that will go under the grill. Mix together soured cream or yoghurt and milk powder, then pour over the pepper mixture, top with breadcrumbs and a few thin flakes of butter, and put under grill until golden and crisp.

In this dish the complementary protein effect comes from the combination of sunflower seeds and skim milk.

Creamy Cauliflower
This is very quick to make. When I'm in a hurry I serve it with a tomato and watercress salad for a quick meal in half an hour.
Serves 4
Calories: 280

1 cauliflower, washed and broken into florets
300g (10 fl oz) soured cream or soft white cheese such as quark
salt and freshly ground black pepper

50g (2 oz) soft wholewheat breadcrumbs
50g (2 oz) grated cheese
a little butter

Put 6mm (¼ inch) water into a medium-sized saucepan or flameproof casserole and bring to the boil. Add the cauliflower, bring back to the boil, put a lid on the pan and simmer for 4–5 minutes, until the cauliflower is tender. Drain. Add the soured cream and some seasoning, mashing the cauliflower a little. If necessary, transfer mixture to a dish which will go under the grill. Top with breadcrumbs, grated cheese and a few flakes of butter and make crisp under the grill.

I've used cauliflower in this recipe because it is quick to prepare and cook, but many other vegetables can be used instead – courgettes, leeks, Jerusalem artichokes, onions or mushrooms, for instance.

Buckwheat and Mushrooms
Serves 4
Calories: 260

225g (8 oz) roasted buckwheat
300ml (½ pint) water
2 teaspoons yeast extract
1 tablespoon tomato purée
2 large onions, chopped
2 sticks celery, diced

1 tablespoon olive oil
4 garlic cloves, crushed
350g (12 oz) dark, open
   mushrooms, washed and
   sliced
salt, pepper and tamari

Put the buckwheat into a saucepan with the water, yeast extract and tomato purée and bring to the boil. Cover with a lid, turn the heat right down and leave for 15 minutes, until buckwheat is fluffy and all the water has been absorbed. Meanwhile fry the onions and celery in the oil for 10 minutes, until soft, then add the garlic and mushrooms and fry for a further 3–4 minutes. Then fork the cooked buckwheat gently into the mixture. Season with salt, pepper and a bit more yeast extract or some tamari if necessary – buckwheat is rather bland and needs plenty of flavour; the cooked buckwheat is also nice with a well-flavoured garlicky tomato sauce.

Bulgur Wheat Pilaff with Carrots, Nuts and Raisins
Bulgur is wheat which has been cracked and steamed. It takes 15 minutes to prepare – as opposed to 45 minutes for brown rice – and is therefore especially useful for quick meals.
Serves 4–6
Calories: 325–490

225g (8 oz) bulgur wheat
600ml (1 pint) boiling water
½ teaspoon salt
1 onion, peeled and chopped
1 small red pepper, deseeded
   and chopped

225g (8 oz) carrots, scraped and
   diced
1 tablespoon ghee or olive oil
1 teaspoon cinnamon
125g (4 oz) flaked almonds
125g (4 oz) raisins

Put the wheat into a large bowl with the water and salt. Cover and leave for 15 minutes. Meanwhile, fry the onion, pepper and carrots in the oil for 10 minutes, then add the cinnamon and stir for a moment or two. Drain the bulgur wheat and add to the onion and pepper, together with the almonds and raisins. Stir gently over the heat for 5–10 minutes, until wheat is heated through, then check seasoning and serve.

Millet and Courgette Risotto

Millet, which you can buy at health food shops, cooks in 20 minutes and has an attractive pale golden colour and a pleasant flavour which makes a change from rice.
Serves 4
Calories: 250

2 onions, peeled and chopped
1 red pepper, deseeded and
   chopped
500g (1 lb) courgettes, sliced
2 garlic cloves, crushed

2 teaspoons ghee or olive oil
250g (8 oz) millet
600ml (1 pint) water
seasoning

Fry the onions, pepper, courgettes and garlic in the ghee or oil in a medium-sized saucepan for 10 minutes. Then add the millet and water and bring to the boil. Cover, turn the heat down and leave to cook for 20 minutes, when millet should be fluffy and water absorbed.

Curry and Brown Rice

The rice will take about 45 minutes to cook, so get this started (see Too-tired-to-cook-rice, page 60) before you begin to make the curry.

Serves 4

Calories: 65 for curried vegetable part; allow extra for rice (100 for 25g/1 oz, uncooked weight)

1 onion, chopped
2 tablespoons ghee
2 teaspoons each turmeric, ground coriander and cumin
450g (1 lb) mixed vegetables: carrot, cut into rings; potato, swede, diced; celery, leeks, sliced; cauliflower, broken into largish sprigs

1 garlic clove, crushed
1 bay leaf
300ml (½ pint) water
250g (8 oz) tomatoes, skinned and chopped
salt and paper
hot cooked brown rice, made from 225g (8 oz) raw weight, to serve

Fry the onion in the ghee for 10 minutes, then add the spices and fry for 1–2 minutes. Put in the vegetables and garlic and stir, so they're coated with the fat and spices, then add the bay leaf, water and tomatoes. Bring to the boil, cover and cook gently until the vegetables are tender – 15–20 minutes. Season and serve with the cooked rice.

Curry can be one of the most festive of meals if you have fun with all the colourful trimmings placed round the main dish in little bowls. Here are some suggestions: mango chutney, lime pickle, sliced bananas sprinkled with lemon juice, peeled and sliced oranges, sliced tomato, roasted peanuts, sliced hard-boiled egg, desiccated coconut, diced cucumber in yoghurt, onions sliced and marinated in vinaigrette with paprika and poppy seed. And don't forget the poppodums – you can buy them from most supermarkets or Indian shops. Raw, they look like rounds of wafer but when grilled they swell to twice their original size and are crisp, savoury and delicious.

Wendy's Black-Eyed Beans
Serves 4
Calories: 230

2 onions, peeled and sliced
2 garlic cloves, crushed
½ teaspoon mixed herbs
½ teaspoon marjoram

1 tablespoon olive oil
225g (8 oz) black-eyed beans
wholewheat breadcrumbs
grated cheese

Fry onions, garlic and herbs in the oil for 5 minutes, then add the beans and water to cover. Simmer gently, lid on pan, until beans are tender (about 35 minutes – keep an eye on the water level and add more if necessary), then liquidize, mash or mouli. Put into a greased oven dish, cover generously with breadcrumbs, sprinkle with a little grated cheese and grill until the top is crunchy.

Here the bean protein is complemented by the wheat and cheese protein to make sure you're not missing out on anything. This recipe can also be made with aduki beans, for a change.

Too-tired-to-cook Rice
This is what I make when the last thing I feel like doing is cooking. I put the rice on to cook, then go away and do something else for about 30 minutes. Then, 10 minutes before the rice is due to be cooked, I prepare the mushroom mixture and a green salad. The whole meal is ready in about 45 minutes, with biscuits and cheese, fruit or yoghurt for pudding. (And for an alternative way of cooking and serving this rice dish, see aubergine and tomato casserole, page 66.)
Serves 4
Calories: 300

225g (8 oz) long grain brown rice

500ml (1 pint) water

1 level teaspoon sea salt

225g (8 oz) button mushrooms

15g (½ oz) butter

50g (2 oz) sunflower seeds

Put the rice, water and salt into a pan (with a lid) and bring to the boil. Boil hard for 5 minutes, then put the lid on and turn heat right down. Leave for 40 minutes. Meanwhile fry the mushrooms in the butter. Fork up the rice when cooked, add sunflower seeds and serve with the mushrooms and their liquid poured over.

The protein in the sunflower seeds complements the rice protein and adds a pleasant 'bite'.

I think it's always worth cooking some extra rice. It will keep for several days in the fridge and can form the basis of a number of other dishes. A rice salad, for instance, like the ones on pages 49 and 50, or, with the addition of a fried onion, a few mushrooms, some herbs (marjoram, say?) and perhaps a little tomato purée, it makes a very savoury filling for parboiled courgettes, marrow or peppers. Altogether a very good friend.

West Indian Red Beans

Serves 4

Calories: 250 (allow extra for rice, 100 calories per 25g/1 oz, uncooked weight)

225g (8 oz) red kidney beans, soaked in cold water overnight or in boiling water for 2 hours

1 large onion, sliced

1 carrot, sliced

1 garlic clove, crushed

2 heaped teaspoons thyme

75g (3 oz) creamed coconut

salt and pepper

hot cooked brown rice, made from 225g (8 oz) raw weight, to serve

Rinse beans, then put into a saucepan with the onion, carrot, garlic and thyme. Boil for 10 minutes, then turn the heat down and leave to simmer until tender, 1–1½ hours. Stir in creamed coconut and allow to melt. This adds a delicious sweetness to the dish and thickens it a bit, too. Season with salt and pepper. Serve hot with brown rice for a very filling and well-balanced meal – beans and rice complement each other protein-wise.

Wholewheat Spaghetti with Lentil Sauce

When funds allow, some cheapish red wine, such as a Bulgarian Cabernet Sauvignon, goes very well with this: add a couple of tablespoons to the sauce before serving, too.

Serves 4

Calories: 380 without grated cheese

1 onion, peeled and chopped
1 small red pepper, deseeded and chopped
2 tablespoons olive oil
1 garlic clove, crushed
1 teaspoon dried basil
225g (8 oz) can tomatoes
125g (4 oz) split red lentils
1 tablespoon tomato purée
400ml (¾ pint) water

salt and pepper
sugar
225g (8 oz) wholewheat spaghetti or rings
15g (½ oz) butter
grated cheese to serve, optional (25g/1 oz hard cheddar is 120 calories, Parmesan is 110, reduced-fat hard cheeses 60–70)

Fry the onion and pepper in the oil in a large saucepan for 10 minutes, then put in the garlic, basil, tomatoes, lentils, purée and water. Bring to the boil, then turn the heat down and leave to simmer gently, uncovered, for 15–20 minutes, until the lentils are cooked. Season with salt, pepper and a dash of sugar. About 15 minutes before the sauce is ready, start cooking the pasta. Half-fill a large saucepan with lightly salted water and bring to the boil. Add the pasta, easing spaghetti down into the water as the ends soften. Boil rapidly, uncovered, for about 10 minutes, until a piece feels just tender when you bite it. Drain, then return to the pan with the butter and salt and pepper to taste. Serve with the sauce and hand round grated cheese, if you're using this. Some watercress or green salad is nice with it, too.

Here, the wheat in the pasta combines with the lentils in the sauce to make an excellent protein dish.

Tofu Fritters with Lemon

Meat-eaters compare this to fried fish. Delicious with the yoghurt dressing on page 36, or parsley sauce (as on page 79, but with 2–3 tablespoons chopped parsley instead of cheese), and a salad or quickly cooked vegetable. You need to allow time for the tofu to drain.

Serves 4
Calories: 280

2 300g (10 oz) packets tofu, from health shops
salt, pepper and lemon juice
wholewheat flour

olive oil or ghee for shallow-frying
lemon wedges

Drain the tofu carefully, being careful not to break it up. Then wrap each block of tofu in a clean absorbent cloth, place in a colander and arrange a weight on top. Leave for several hours – overnight and during the following day if possible – to drain and firm up. Then cut into slices, sprinkle each with salt, pepper and a few drops of lemon juice and coat in flour. Shallow-fry until crisp and golden brown on both sides. Drain on kitchen paper. Serve at once, with the lemon wedges.

Cauliflower with Spicy Peanut Sauce
Serves 4
Calories: 280

1 large cauliflower

salt

For the sauce
1 onion, peeled and chopped
1 tablespoon olive oil
1 tablespoon peanut butter
125g (4 oz) roasted peanuts (see
   page 115), chopped or grated

450g (1 lb) tomatoes, skinned
   and chopped
pepper

Start by making the sauce. Fry the onion in the oil for 10
minutes, then add the peanut butter, peanuts and tomatoes.
Season and keep warm. Wash and trim the cauliflower,
dividing it into small florets as you do so. Heat 2cm (1 inch)
salted water in a saucepan, put in the cauliflower and cook for
about 5 minutes, until tender. Serve cauliflower with the sauce
spooned over it.

Chickpeas and Pasta
Serves 4
Calories: 430

225g (8 oz) chickpeas, soaked
   overnight
175g (6 oz) wholewheat pasta
   rings
1 garlic clove, crushed

4 tablespoons olive oil
chopped parsley
salt and freshly ground black
   pepper

Drain and rinse the chickpeas; put into a pan with plenty of
cold water and simmer gently for 2–2½ hours, until tender. 10–

15 minutes before they're ready, half-fill a large saucepan with water and bring to the boil. Put in the pasta rings and cook, uncovered, for about 10 minutes, until they're just tender. Drain and add the crushed garlic, oil and the drained chickpeas. Season with a little salt and plenty of freshly ground black pepper. Sprinkle with chopped-parsley and serve with a green salad or a tomato salad.

This is a suprisingly good mixture and, again, contains complementary proteins for first-class nourishment. (It sounds fattening, but remember it's a complete meal you've got there, and the salad that's served with it won't add many calories to the meal as long as it's lightly dressed with lemon juice and just a touch of oil.)

OVEN DISHES

Mushroom Pâté
Serves 4–6
Calories: 280–420

butter and dried crumbs*, wheat germ or oatmeal, for coating tin
450g (1 lb) mushrooms, washed
1 onion, peeled
15g (½ oz) butter
125g (4 oz) milled brazil nuts

225g (8 oz) soft wholewheat bread without crusts
2 tablespoons skim milk powder or soya flour
1 teaspoon yeast extract
1 teaspoon mixed herbs
1 free-range egg
salt and pepper

Set the oven to 180°C (350°F), gas mark 4. Grease a 450g (1 lb)

*Make these by laying slices of wholemeal bread on a baking sheet, drying out in a cool oven until completely crisp, then crushing; store in an airtight tin or jar.

loaf tin and line with a long strip of greased non-stick paper. Sprinkle inside of tin with dried crumbs, wheat germ or oatmeal. Chop mushrooms and onion (quickly done in a food processor) and fry together gently in the butter until tender – 10 minutes. Put mixture back into the food processor with remaining ingredients (bread broken into chunks) and whizz until blended. Or, liquidize mushrooms and onions, grate the brazil nuts and make bread into crumbs, then mix everything together in a bowl. Season. Spoon mixture into prepared tin and bake for 1 hour. Slip a knife round the edges of the loaf to loosen, then turn out. Serve in slices with gravy (pages 67–8), roast potatoes and vegetables. It also slices well when cold and is good with salad or as a filling for sandwiches.

This recipe makes use of the complementary protein in brazil nuts and mushrooms, and in wholewheat bread and skim milk powder (or soya flour), with an egg thrown in as well, to make a nutritious and tasty main dish.

Aubergine and Tomato Casserole
Serves 4
Calories: 70

2 large aubergines
2 large onions, peeled and
  sliced
5 tomatoes, peeled and sliced

2 heaped tablespoons tomato
  purée
salt, pepper and a dash of
  sugar

Set oven to 180°C (350°F), gas mark 4. Wash aubergines, cut into fairly thin, even-sized rounds. Cover with boiling water and leave for 5 minutes; drain. Put aubergines into a buttered casserole with all the other ingredients; cover and bake for 1 hour. This recipe will contribute its own 'gravy' to the meal and goes well with baked potatoes, grated cheese and a green vegetable or side salad; green salad; or as a vegetable accompaniment to another main dish; for instance you could

serve it with the Too-tired-to-cook rice (page 60), in which cas\
the rice can be cooked in the oven too, thus saving power.

A leek and tomato casserole can be made in exactly the same way, substituting leeks for aubergines, and forgetting about the boiling water treatment (which is to remove bitterness from the aubergines).

Chunky Nut and Vegetable Roast

This nut roast has a pleasant, chewy texture.
Serves 4–6
Calories: 270–400

1 carrot, scraped
1 onion, peeled
1 celery stick
225g (8 oz) mixed nuts: for instance, almonds, peanuts, brazil nuts
2 teaspoons yeast extract

2 free-range eggs
1–2 teaspoons dried mixed herbs
salt and pepper
butter and dried crumbs*, wheat germ or oatmeal, for coating tin

Set oven to 190°C (375°F), gas mark 5. Put all the ingredients into a food processor and process until vegetables and nuts are chopped into chunky pieces. Or spread the vegetables and nuts out on a large board and chop with an autochop, then put into a bowl and mix with the remaining ingredients. Line a 450g (1 lb) loaf tin with a strip of non-stick paper. Grease well and sprinkle with dry crumbs. Spoon nut mixture into tin, level top. Bake, uncovered, for 45 minutes, until centre is set. Slip a knife round the edge and turn loaf out on to a warm serving dish. It's good with vegetarian gravy (made by frying a chopped onion, garlic clove and 2 tablespoons flour in 2 tablespoons ghee until nut brown, then adding 400ml/¾ pint water or stock and

---

* See footnote on page 65.

yeast extract, salt and pepper and simmering for 10–15 minutes) and cooked vegetables, or cold with yoghurt dressing (page 36) and salad.

Herby Sunflower Seed Pudding
Serves 4–6
Calories: 240–360

175g (6 oz) wholewheat bread without crusts
125g (4 oz) sunflower seeds
250ml (½ pint) milk
25g (1 oz) butter
1 large onion, peeled and chopped

2 heaped teaspoons mixed herbs
1 free-range egg
salt and freshly ground black pepper

Set oven to 180°C (350°F), gas mark 4. Crumble bread and grind sunflower seeds together, in a food processor or liquidizer. Heat milk and butter together until butter is melted, then mix everything together, seasoning as required. Pour into a greased casserole and bake for 45–60 minutes. Serve with gravy (see above) and vegetables.

In this recipe the protein in the seeds, wholewheat bread and milk is all complementary, making a first-class protein dish.

Easy Pasta and Cheese Bake
This is a real standby because it only takes about 10 minutes to prepare and can be left in a pre-set oven to cook so that its savoury aroma will greet you on your return. If you also leave some green salad washed and ready in the fridge you can have a complete meal on the table in a few minutes.
Serves 4
Calories: 340

4 large onions, chopped
2 teaspoons ghee
175g (6 oz) wholewheat pasta
  rings

700g (1½ lb) tomatoes, skinned
  and chopped, or 2 400g (14
  oz) cans
125g (4 oz) grated cheese

Set oven to 150°C (300°F), gas mark 2. (If pre-setting it, timeit for 2 hours.) Peel and slice onions. Using a pan or flameproofcasserole, fry in the butter for 5 minutes. If necessary transferto an oven dish. Put uncooked pasta rings in an even layer ontop and then tomatoes on top of that, making sure that the pastais covered. Sprinkle with the grated cheese. Cover and bake for2 hours. Serve with a green salad.

Wholewheat pasta and cheese protein combine to make anourishing meal.

Sunflower Seed Hotpot

Serves 4–6
Calories: 240–350

3 large potatoes
125g (4 oz) sunflower seeds
125g (4 oz) wholewheat bread
1 large onion, peeled and
  chopped

2 teaspoons mixed herbs
salt and freshly ground black
  pepper
250ml (½ pint) skim milk
15g (½ oz) butter

Set oven to 150°C (300°F), gas mark 2. (If pre-setting it, timeit for 2 hours.) Peel potatoes and slice into thin rounds; sprinklewith a little salt. Grind sunflower seeds and bread together, ina food processor or liquidizer; mix with the onion, herbs anda little seasoning. Layer potatoes and sunflower seed mixtureinto a greased casserole, ending with potatoes, then pour in themilk. Dot with the butter. Cover and bake for 2 hours,removing the cover for the last 15–20 minutes, to brown thetop. Serve with a green vegetable and gravy (see pages 67–8).

Wheat (in the bread), potatoes, sunflower seeds and milk area good protein combination.

Lazy Lentils

This is blissfully simple because you don't even have to soak the lentils beforehand, let alone cook them in advance.
Serves 4–6
Calories: 200–300

4 large onions, peeled and chopped
1 tablespoon olive oil
1 garlic clove, crushed
250ml (½ pint) water
2 teaspoons yeast extract

175g (6 oz) split red lentils
1 teaspoon mixed herbs
salt and freshly ground black pepper
125g (4 oz) grated cheese
breadcrumbs

Set oven to 150°C (300°F), gas mark 3. (If pre-setting it, time it for 2 hours.) Using if possible a flameproof casserole, fry the onions in the butter for 5–7 minutes, browning lightly, then add the garlic, water and yeast extract and stir until yeast extract has dissolved. Take off heat and add lentils, herbs, seasoning and most of the cheese. Sprinkle rest of cheese on top, together with some crumbs, then bake for 2 hours. Serve with vegetables and gravy (pages 67–8) or a parsley sauce.

The protein in the lentils and the cheese is complementary.

TWO-OUT-OF-ONE DISHES

Once the basic preparation has been done, some of these recipes are very quick indeed and can make fast suppers if the basic mix is in the fridge.

Continental (Green) Lentils

BASIC MIXTURE

300g (12 oz) large continental (green) lentils

Cover lentils generously with cold water and soak for 2–8 hours. Drain and rinse lentils, put into a pan, cover with their height again in cold water. Bring to the boil and simmer gently for 30–40 minutes, until tender. Drain, but keep liquid. Use to make:

1. SHEPHERDS PIE
Serves 4
Calories: 340

2 onions, chopped
1 tablespoon ghee or olive oil
2 garlic cloves, crushed
⅔ basic cooked continental
  lentils

1–2 teaspoons mixed herbs
1 teaspoon yeast extract
salt and pepper
700g (1½ lb) mashed potatoes

Set oven to 200°C (400°F), gas mark 6. Fry the onions in the ghee or oil for 10 minutes, browning lightly. Remove from heat and add garlic, lentils, herbs and yeast extract. Add enough of reserved cooking liquid (see basic mixture, above) to make a soft consistency. Season, then spoon mixture into a shallow ovenproof dish and spread mashed potatoes on top. Rough up with a fork. Bake for 35–40 minutes.

2. CONTINENTAL LENTIL BURGERS
Serves 4
Calories: 280

1 onion, finely chopped
1 tablespoon ghee or olive oil
⅓ basic continental lentil
   mixture
125g (4 oz) light wholewheat
   breadcrumbs
1 garlic clove, crushed

1 teaspoon mixed herbs
1 teaspoon yeast extract
salt and freshly ground black
   pepper
wholewheat flour for coating
olive oil for shallow-frying

Fry the onion in the ghee or oil for 10 minutes, then add the lentils (make sure they're well drained), the breadcrumbs, garlic, herbs, yeast extract and salt and pepper to taste. Form into 8 flat burgers, coat in wholewheat flour and fry in hot olive oil until crisp and brown on both sides. Drain on kitchen paper. They're nice in soft burger-buns with chutney or salad; or with mayonnaise or natural yoghurt and some crisp salad.

Split Peas

BASIC MIXTURE

500g (1 lb 2 oz) split peas
1 large onion, sliced

2 cloves

Put the split peas, onion and cloves into a saucepan and cook gently until split peas are tender – about 30 minutes. Remove cloves and divide mixture in half, using one batch to make curried split peas and the other for pease pudding bake.

1. CURRIED SPLIT PEAS
Serves 4
Calories: 260; allow extra for rice (25g/1 oz uncooked weight is 100 calories)

1 large onion, peeled and
  chopped
2 apples, peeled and chopped
2 teaspoons ghee or olive oil
1 tablespoon curry powder
½ basic split pea mixture,
  above

50g (2 oz) sultanas
cooked brown rice, made from
  225g (8 oz) raw weight, and
  desiccated coconut to serve

Fry the onion and apple in the ghee or oil until tender and lightly browned; add curry powder and cook for another couple of minutes. Then add the split pea mixture, sultanas and a little water if necessary to make the consistency you want. Heat through, season and serve with the brown rice, sprinkled with a little desiccated coconut.

The rice and split peas supply complementary proteins, making this a potent combination.

2. PEASE PUDDING
Serves 4
Calories: 220

1 large onion, chopped
1 tablespoon ghee or olive oil
1 teaspoon sage
½ basic split pea mixture

salt and freshly ground black
  pepper
ghee or a few flakes of butter

Set the oven to 200°C (400°F), gas mark 6. Fry the onion in the ghee or oil for 10 minutes, then add the sage and cook for 2–3 minutes more. Add basic split pea mixture, season, then spread mixture into a shallow casserole. Top with a little ghee or a few flakes of butter. Bake for 30 minutes. Nice served with mint sauce (chopped fresh mint mixed with wine vinegar and a dash of honey), potatoes and vegetables, or sliced cold, with salad.

To make the most of the protein in the split peas, serve this dish with a little cheese or milk protein – potatoes mashed with milk, or a vegetable in a white sauce, for instance; or what about ending the meal with yoghurt or biscuits and cheese? (That's the fun of this sort of cookery – there's plenty of scope for menu-building, and when it means saving money and resources, it's well worthwhile.)

Chickpeas

Here you have a hot and a cold chickpea dish, two very different end products.

BASIC MIXTURE

500g (1 lb 2 oz) chickpeas   water

Cover chickpeas generously with cold water and soak overnight; or bring to the boil, then remove from heat, cover and leave to soak for 1 hour. In either case, rinse the chickpeas, cover with their height again in cold water, bring to the boil and simmer gently until tender: takes 1–2 hours. Then drain (keeping cooking water) and divide into two equal portions.

1. HOT GARLIC CHICKPEAS IN PITTA BREAD
Serves 4–6
Calories: 270–400; allow 140 calories for a piece of pitta bread

½ quantity cooked chickpeas
self-raising wholewheat flour to
   coat
salt and pepper
4 tablespoons ghee

2 tablespoons olive oil
2–4 garlic cloves, crushed
4–6 pieces warm wholewheat
   pitta bread to serve

Spread chickpeas out on a large plate and sprinkle with the flour and a little salt and pepper. Turn them gently so that each one is coated with flour. Heat ghee and oil in a large frying pan; add chickpeas and garlic. Fry chickpeas gently until crisp and golden, turning them often. You may need to do them in more than one batch. Slit open the tops of the pitta bread, fill with the hot chickpeas and serve immediately. Some sliced firm tomatoes and mild onion rings are nice in the pitta bread with the chickpeas, and a dollop of natural yoghurt on top makes a pleasant finishing touch. Serve with a crisp green salad for more of a meal.

The protein here is excellent: chickpeas and wheat combining to give first-class nourishment, with extra help from the yoghurt if you serve it.

2. HUMMUS
Serves 4–8
Calories: 150 if serving 8; 200 if serving 6; 300 if serving 4

½ quantity cooked chickpeas
2 garlic cloves, crushed
4 teaspoons tahini
2 tablespoons olive oil
2 tablespoons lemon juice
240 ml (8–9 fl oz) reserved
  cooking liquid

salt and pepper
extra olive oil, paprika pepper,
  lemon slices, black olives,
  warm wholewheat pitta
  bread to serve

Put chickpeas into food processor or liquidizer with the garlic, tahini, olive oil, lemon juice and a little of the cooking liquid. Blend until smooth, adding enough of the cooking liquid to make the consistency of lightly whipped cream. Season with salt and pepper. Then spread mixture out on a flat plate or four individual ones, so that it's about 1cm (½ inch) deep. Pour the remaining olive oil on top, sprinkle with paprika and garnish with slices of lemon and black olives. Serve with warm wholewheat pitta bread as a filling first course or snack.

This is a wonderful example of complementary proteins at

work in an age-old traditional dish. The tahini, chickpeas and wheat all combine to make excellent protein. Nothing lacking here!

Basic Wholewheat Pastry Mix

Pastry, with its high fat content, isn't the healthiest thing you can eat, but it is delicious, and if you use wholemeal flour and keep to low-fat dishes for the rest of the day's eating, there's no reason why you shouldn't enjoy it sometimes!

BASIC MIX

350g (12 oz) plain wholemeal flour   4–5 tablespoons cold water
175g (6 oz) butter

Sift flour into a bowl, adding the residue of bran left behind in the sieve. Rub in the butter with your fingertips until the mixture looks like fine breadcrumbs. Add the water to make a dough. Divide in half and use one lot to make a pastry pizza and the other for a savoury onion flan.

1. PASTRY PIZZA
Serves 4
Calories: 400

½ basic pastry mix

For the topping
2 onions, peeled and finely
  chopped
2 teaspoons ghee or olive oil
1½ tablespoons concentrated
  tomato purée

salt and pepper
40g (1½ oz) grated cheese
1 heaped teaspoon oregano

Set oven to 220°C (425°F), gas mark 7. Roll out pastry and use to line a flat dish or pizza plate. Prick lightly all over. Chill while you make the topping. Fry the onion in the ghee or oil for 10 minutes, until soft. Remove from heat and add the tomato purée and seasoning. Spread onion mixture over pastry, sprinkle with the grated cheese and oregano. Bake for 15–20 minutes. Serve with a crisp green salad.

2. SAVOURY ONION TART
Serves 6
Calories: 310

½ basic pastry mix	1 free-range egg
2 onions, chopped	150ml (5 fl oz) milk
sea salt	75g (3 oz) grated cheese

Set oven to 200°C (400°F), gas mark 6. Roll out pastry and use to line a 20cm (8 inch) flan tin. Chill. Boil the onions in a little sea-salted water until nearly tender, drain well. Beat together the egg and milk, add onions and cheese and pour into flan. Bake for 10 minutes, then turn down oven setting to 180°C (350°F), gas mark 4, and bake for a further 30 minutes. Serve hot.

Red Beans
Like the chickpea two-out-of-one, this recipe gives a hot and a cold dish.

BASIC MIXTURE

500g (1 lb 2 oz) red kidney beans   water

Cover the beans generously with cold water and soak overnight, or bring them to the boil then cover and soak for 1 hour. Either way, then drain and rinse. Add fresh water to cover the beans by their height again, then bring to the boil and boil fiercely for

10 minutes. Then cover, turn the heat down, and leave beans to simmer gently for 1–1½ hours, until tender. Divide into two portions.

1. RED BEAN SALAD
Serves 4–6
Calories: 165–250

½ quantity of cooked red kidney beans, still hot if possible
1 onion, chopped
1 garlic clove, crushed
1 tablespoon wine vinegar
2–3 tablespoons olive oil
1 tablespoon tomato ketchup or purée
salt, pepper and a dash of molasses sugar

Just mix everything together, turning the beans well so they're all coated and seasoning with a little salt, pepper and (if you're using the purée) a dash of sugar to taste. Leave for at least 2 hours, stirring occasionally. It's lovely with warm wholewheat rolls or a wholewheat stick and some watercress, and if you serve it like this you'll have the bean-wheat protein combination going for you for first-class nourishment.

2. RED BEAN MOUSSAKA

For a simpler version of this dish, leave out the aubergine, sprinkle the bean mixture with crumbs and bake as it is.

Serves 6
Calories: 400

2 medium-sized aubergines (about 500g/1 lb) sliced into 6mm (¼ inch) circles
1 large onion, peeled and chopped
5 tablespoons olive oil
½ quantity of red beans
4 tomatoes
1 tablespoon tomato purée
1–2 tablespoons red wine (optional)

½ teaspoon allspice or cinnamon
salt, pepper and molasses sugar
1 egg
400ml (¾ pint) cheese sauce (see below)
50g (2 oz) grated cheese

Sprinkle aubergine circles with salt, place in a colander with a plate and a weight on top and leave for 30 minutes. Then rinse under the cold tap and squeeze dry. Set oven to 180°C (350°F), gas mark 4. Fry the onion in 1 tablespoon of the oil for 10 minutes, then add beans, tomatoes, purée and wine, mashing the beans a little. Add allspice or cinnamon and season with salt, pepper and a dash of sugar if necessary. Fry the aubergine slices in the remaining oil and pat on kitchen paper to remove excess oil. Beat the egg into the cheese sauce. Grease a shallow ovenproof dish; put half aubergine slices into base of dish, cover with half the red bean mixture and then half the sauce. Repeat layers, ending with the sauce, then sprinkle the top with grated cheese. Bake for 1 hour.

To make the cheese sauce, put 40g (1½ oz) butter, 1½ tablespoons cornflour or arrowroot and 400ml (¾ pint) milk into a pan and whisk over the heat until thickened. Remove from heat, stir in 50g (2 oz) grated cheese and season to taste.

Another powerful protein combination, with the bean protein made more potent by that in the milk, cheese and egg.

British Field Beans

It's well worth getting to know field beans if you see them; they're cheap and can be very tasty if they're well chopped (in a food processor) after cooking to break down the skins. If you can't get field beans, use black or brown beans for this two-out-of-one.

BASIC MIXTURE

500g (1 lb 2 oz) British field beans   water

Soak the beans in plenty of cold water overnight. Next day drain and rinse beans, put into a saucepan with their height again in cold water, boil vigorously for 10 minutes, then simmer gently for 30–60 minutes, until tender. Drain, reserving liquid.

1. FIELD BEAN BURGERS
Serves 4–6
Calories: 280–400

1 onion, chopped
2 teaspoons ghee or olive oil
2 garlic cloves, crushed
⅔ quantity of basic cooked field
  beans

4 tablespoons chopped parsley
1 tablespoon lemon juice
salt and pepper
flour and a little ghee or oil to
  coat

Fry the onion in the ghee or oil for 5 minutes, then add the garlic and fry for a further 5 minutes. Chop beans in food processor until reduced to a coarse purée. Add onion and garlic, parsley, lemon juice and seasoning. Coat with flour, then brush with ghee or oil and grill or bake in a moderate oven until crisp on both sides, turning halfway through cooking time.

Serve in a soft wholewheat bap, with pickles; or as part of a cooked meal, with parsley sauce or a yoghurt pudding to supply some complementary protein.

2. FIELD BEAN PÂTÉ
Serves 4
Calories: 125

⅓ cooked field beans
2 garlic cloves, chopped
bunch of parsley

1 tablespoon wine vinegar
4 teaspoons olive oil
seasoning

Put all ingredients into food processor and whizz to a coarse purée, adding enough of the reserved cooking liquid to make a consistency like softly whipped cream. Spoon into a bowl. This is delicious served with fingers of hot wholewheat toast, or used as a sandwich spread and, in each case, the wheat protein complements that in the beans to give you great value.

Dried Chestnuts

BASIC MIXTURE

500g (1 lb 2 oz) dried chestnuts   water

Soak the chestnuts in plenty of cold water overnight. Next day, put into a pan with enough water to cover generously and simmer for 2–3 hours, until tender, adding more water if necessary. Drain, reserving liquid. Use to make a savoury chestnut bake and a chestnut and wine casserole.

1. SAVOURY CHESTNUT BAKE
Serves 6–8
Calories: 290–390

1 onion, peeled and sliced
1 celery stick, chopped
2 teaspoons ghee or olive oil
½ quantity of chestnuts
2 garlic cloves, peeled
125g (4 oz) walnuts, grated

125g (4 oz) cashew nuts, grated
grated rind and juice of ½ lemon
1 glass red wine, optional
1 free-range egg, optional
salt and pepper

Set oven to 190°C (375°F), gas mark 5. Line a 900g (2 lb) loaf tin with a long strip of non-stick paper and brush with ghee or melted butter. Fry the onion and celery in the ghee or olive oil in a large saucepan for 10 minutes. Remove from heat and mix in remaining ingredients, mashing chestnuts so that mixture holds together. Season. Put mixture into the loaf tin – it won't fill it, but is just too much for a 450g (1 lb) tin – and smooth top. Cover with foil and bake for about 45 minutes, removing foil 15 minutes before end of cooking time.

2. CHESTNUT AND WINE CASSEROLE
Serves 4–6
Calories: 250–370

2 large onions, chopped
450g (1 lb) carrots, cut into
  rings
2 tablespoons olive oil
4 garlic cloves, crushed
½ basic chestnuts
10 each of allspice berries,
  juniper berries and black
  peppercorns
1 teaspoon each dried thyme
  and rosemary

575ml (1 pint) vegetable stock
  (page 25)
400ml (¾ pint) cheap red
  wine
1 tablespoon paprika pepper
125g (4 oz) button mushrooms,
  sliced
salt

Fry the onions and carrots in the oil for 10 minutes, then add the garlic, chestnuts, crushed spices, herbs, stock and wine. Bring to the boil, then put a lid on the pan and leave to cook gently for 30–40 minutes, until vegetables are tender, and liquid much reduced and thickened. Then add the paprika and mushrooms. Check seasoning, simmer for a further 2–3 minutes to cook mushrooms, and serve. Jacket potatoes go well with this, and very lightly cooked Brussels sprouts, or a simple crisp green salad.

(Almost) sugarless puddings and sweets

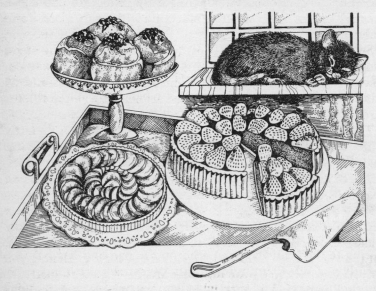

As you have gathered by now, there's a certain amount of colour discrimination in wholefood cookery – all that insistence on brown rice, brown flour, brown bread – but nowhere is this more strongly felt than with sugar. Brown sugar, you're told, is good, whereas white sugar is bad. I've known some health food addicts use far more brown sugar than an ordinary family uses white, on the assumption that brown sugar actually does them good. Well, that's a mistake.

Any sugar, brown, white or in between, is fundamentally an unnatural product. Think of sugar as it occurs naturally. It's wrapped up in bulky fruits and vegetables. To get a little sugar you've got to do some chewing. And to get the amount most of us eat every year, you've got to do a mighty lot of chewing. In fact I think it would be an impossibility, given a normal jaw and the usual number of hours in the day. I must say I think that tying sugar up in bulky fruits and vegetables is one of Nature's cleverest tricks. The trouble is, modern machinery and methods of refining have upset things, and now sugar has become a major scourge of our time, responsible for bad teeth, obesity, and having a strong connection with heart disease and diabetes.

So, what's the answer? It isn't easy to do without sugar altogether in family cookery. But it is perfectly possible to cut down on it by having fresh fruit instead of puddings and by using the inherent sweetness of the various natural ingredients in recipes instead of additional sugar.

There are also some interesting findings which have recently come from Russia, which suggest that real raw barbados muscovado sugar isn't such a baddie as the others. Which stands to reason, as it retains a lot more of the original product than its white counterparts.

Honey (from a beekeeper using proper organic methods, not feeding the bees on sugar) also has some useful trace elements. It also 'feels' right. I'm sorry to be so unscientific about this, but there are times when, in the absence of hard evidence, you simply have to trust your instincts about food. (I'm glad, for instance, that I and other wholefooders trusted our feelings about wholemeal flour and bread in the days before the magic 'fibre' was discovered and some doctors and nutritionists used to laugh at us for our misguided prejudice. 'By all means keep your wholemeal bread, if you want to, dear,' said one to me, 'but don't get any silly ideas that it's any better for you than white' . . .)

But to come back to this sugar question. Since (like any other pure sugar) neither honey nor real barbados sugar have any of the vital fibre (which means they pass into the bloodstream too quickly, causing the need for a massive rush on insulin), both should still be used in strict moderation.

So in this section you'll find puddings which rely mainly on the natural sweetness of ingredients with the occasional touch of honey or raw sugar.

85

Stewed Apple and Date
Serves 4
Calories: 150

450g (1 lb) cooking apples   2 tablespoons water
175g (6 oz) cooking dates

Peel, core and slice apples. Chop dates. Cook together in the water until apples are light and fluffy. Serve warm or chilled. Nice with the cashew nut cream on page 113. An apple and blackberry variation of this is pleasant, too: use 225g (8 oz) blackberries instead of the dates, and sweeten with a little honey or soft brown sugar.

Healthy Apple Crumble
Serves 6
Calories: 350

Use the above mixture. Put into an ovenproof dish and top with either a layer of Jordan's Crunchy (from health shops) or a wholemeal crumble mix made by sifting 225g (8 oz) plain wholewheat flour with 2 teaspoons of baking powder and rubbing in 75g (3 oz) unsalted butter. Then fork in 75g (3 oz) raw barbados sugar. Bake for 30–40 minutes at 180°C (350°F), gas mark 4.

Baked Apples with Raisins
Serves 4
Calories: 175

4 medium-sized cooking
  apples
125g (4 oz) raisins

1 tablespoon honey
6 tablespoons hot water

Set oven to 190°C (375°F), gas mark 5. Core the apples; score the skin around the middles. Stuff the centres with the raisins. Dissolve the honey in the water. Put the apples into a lightly greased casserole dish, pour the honey mixture round them. Bake in a moderate oven for about 40 minutes.

Continental Apple Tart
Serves 6
Calories: 320

700g (1½ lb) sweet apples –
  Cox's are ideal
2 tablespoons water
125g (4 oz) raisins
honey

18cm (7 inch) pastry flan case
  (see below), cooked
1–2 tablespoons clear honey

Set oven to 190°C (375°F), gas mark 5. Peel, core and dice half the apples; simmer gently in the water with the raisins until tender. Sweeten with a little honey if necessary. Cool, then spread over flan case. Peel, core and thinly slice rest of apples; arrange on top of flan. Brush with honey. Bake for about 30 minutes, until apple slices are cooked and lightly browned. Serve warm.

    To make the flan case, rub 75g (3 oz) unsalted butter into 150g (6 oz) plain wholewheat flour then mix to a dough with 6 teaspoons cold water. Roll out and line an 18cm (7 inch) flan tin; trim, prick base all over and bake at 200°C (400°F), gas mark 6, for 20 minutes.

Date Tart
Something like a healthy version of a treacle tart!
Serves 6
Calories: 380

350g (12 oz) dates
150ml (5 fl oz) water
grated rind of an orange
18cm (7 inch) wholemeal flan
  case, baked (see page 87)

25g (1 oz) chopped almonds or
  a little desiccated coconut

Set oven to 190°C (375°F), gas mark 5. Chop dates roughly, put into a saucepan with the water and simmer gently until thick and purée-like. Remove from heat, add the orange rind. Spoon mixture into flan case, level top. Sprinkle with the almonds or coconut. Bake for about 20 minutes, until heated through.

Orange with Creamy Custard Topping
Serves 4
Calories: 175

4 large oranges
1 tablespoon arrowroot
2 free-range egg yolks

250ml (½ pint) skim milk
dash of honey
toasted almonds

Remove skin and pith from oranges; slice into a shallow dish. Make a custard by blending the arrowroot with the egg yolks and a little of the milk. Boil remaining milk, pour over arrowroot mixture, return to pan. Stir over a gentle heat until thickened. Sweeten to taste with a little honey. Pour over oranges; sprinkle with toasted almonds. Serve warm or chilled.

Apricot Fool
Serves 4
Calories: 190

225g (8 oz) dried unsulphured apricots, washed and covered with boiling water, soaked overnight

grated orange rind (optional)
250ml (½ pint) firm natural yoghurt or tofu
dash of honey or raw sugar

After soaking overnight, simmer apricots very gently in their water until really tender. Liquidize with enough of the water to make a thick purée. Add orange rind if using, then mix in the yoghurt or tofu (drain water off tofu first). Sweeten a little as necessary. Serve chilled. Nice with some crunchy toasted flaked almonds scattered on top.

The natural sweetness of chestnuts makes them very suitable for this recipe too. Chestnut fool is made in exactly the same way, using dehydrated chestnuts instead of dried apricots, but you'll need to simmer the chestnuts for about 3 hours to get them tender. Add a dash of brandy or rum, if you like them, instead of the orange rind, for a treat.

Healthy Cheesecake
I invented this for a mid-summer cookery demonstration; since then it's become a firm favourite.
Serves 6–8
Calories: 235–315 with strawberries; 245–330 with grapes

For the base
225g (8 oz) rolled oats
25g (1 oz) flaked almonds
grated rind of a well-scrubbed orange

3 tablespoons clear honey

For the filling

175g (6 oz) quark or firm
  tofu, drained
225g (8 oz) firm yoghurt,
  preferably strained Greek

1 tablespoon honey

To finish

225g (8 oz) ripe strawberries or raspberries, or black grapes, halved
  and stoned, or orange segments, or peach slices sprinkled with
  lemon juice

To make the base, mix all the ingredients together, press into
a 20–22cm (8–9 inch) flan dish. Chill while you make the filling.
Put quark or tofu into a bowl and mix in the yoghurt and honey.
Spoon into flan dish, level top. Arrange fruit on top. Chill for
2–3 hours.

This flan can be varied in many ways. For a carob-banana
flan, replace 25g (1 oz) of the oats with 25g (1 oz) carob powder
and top the cheesecake with sliced bananas sprinked with
lemon juice. Or for a continental-style cheesecake, add 125g (4
oz) raisins to the cheese mixture and finish cheesecake by
sprinkling top with cinnamon instead of the fruit.

Strawberry and Cashew Nut Ice Cream
This is an amazingly good, totally non-dairy ice cream.
Serves 4–6
Calories: 260–390

225g (8 oz) cashew nut pieces
300ml (11 fl oz) water
225g (8 oz) strawberries, stalks
  removed

1 tablespoon clear honey

Put the cashew nuts and water into the food processor or
liquidizer and whizz to a cream. Then add the strawberries and

honey and whizz again. Pour into a polythene container and freeze until solid. Remove from deep freeze a good 30 minutes before you want to eat it.

Eggless Pancakes

This is a useful recipe if you don't eat eggs, and, though I don't think the pancakes have the melting deliciousness of egg-based ones, they are a perfectly satisfactory substitute for them in any sweet or savoury recipe.

Makes about 10, approximately 100 calories each

50g (2 oz) arrowroot	300ml (10 fl oz) water
100g (4 oz) 81% self-raising flour	salt
2 tablespoons olive oil or ghee	extra olive oil or ghee for frying

Sift arrowroot and flour into a bowl. Add the oil or ghee, then gradually beat in the water, adding enough to make a thin, pouring batter, the consistency of single cream. I think this mixture needs a good pinch of salt added, but this is, of course, optional. Heat a little oil or ghee in a small frying pan (you only need a little fat, just to prevent the pancake from sticking), then pour in enough batter to coat the base of the frying pan thinly – about 2 tablespoons – tilting the pan from side to side so the mixture spreads out well. Cook the pancake for a minute or so until the underside is just turning golden and the top is set, then flip it over with a palette knife and cook the other side. Then take the pancake out and put on a plate, piling the rest on top as you make more from the mixture.

Real Fruit Jellies

Very easy to make. Choose your favourite fruit juice, or use 175g (6 oz) dried apricots, soaked overnight in cold water then

whizzed to a purée in the blender, with extra water if necessary to make up to 550ml (1 pint).
Serves 6
Calories: 70–100, depending on type of juice used; about 80 for the apricot version

2 teaspoons gelozone, from
  health shops
550ml (1 pint) fruit juice:
  pineapple, apple, orange or
  grape

a little chopped fruit: apple,
  banana or a few grapes

Put the gelozone into a medium-sized saucepan and mix to a paste with a little of the fruit juice, then gradually blend in the rest. Bring to the boil, stirring, then boil for 1 minute. Remove from the heat. Put the fruit into six individual serving dishes, pour the jelly mixture on top and leave to set. Some cashew nut cream or whipped tofu cream goes very well with this.

Dried Fruit Compote with Cashew Cream
Serves 4–6
Calories: 160–240, without cashew nut cream

450g (1 lb) dried fruit salad
  mix, from health shops

boiling water
cashew nut cream, page 113

Wash the dried fruit well in warm water, then put it into a bowl, cover generously with boiling water and leave to soak for several hours. After that, put the fruit into a saucepan, together with the water in which it was soaked, and simmer gently, without a lid, until the fruit is tender and the water syrupy and much reduced. Cool, then chill. Serve with the cashew nut cream.

Fruit Salad
Serves 4
Calories: 130

125g (4 oz) dried whole
   apricots, from health shops
boiling water
2 large juicy oranges
1 large eating apple, with a rosy
   skin if possible, washed

1 banana
125g (4 oz) grapes, halved and
   stoned

Put the dried apricots into a bowl and cover with boiling water.
Leave to soak for several hours, then stew them gently in a
saucepan, with their soaking water, for about 20 minutes if
necessary, to make them more tender. Cool and put into a bowl.
Hold the oranges over the bowl (to catch the juice) and cut off
the skin, going round and round like peeling an apple. Then
cut the segments of flesh away from the skin and membranes.
Slice the apple, peel and slice the banana, and add to the bowl.
Spoon into individual serving dishes.

Muesli as a Pudding
Serves 4–6
Calories: 205–310

3 large apples, washed and
   grated, skin, core and all
150 ml (5 fl oz) orange juice
125g (4 oz) rolled oats, or a
   mixture of oats and barley
   flakes, from the health shop

1 tablespoon clear honey
50g (2 oz) raisins
50g (2 oz) flaked almonds

Put all the ingredients except the almonds into a bowl and mix
together. Spoon into bowls, sprinkle with the nuts.

Coconut Bananas
Serves 4
Calories: 300

2 bananas
2 oranges
125g (4 oz) coconut cream
150ml (5 fl oz) boiling water

1 teaspoon honey
desiccated coconut or toasted
  coconut strands

Peel and slice bananas; peel, pith and slice oranges; mix fruits together, and put into serving dish(es). Grate creamed coconut, cover with the boiling water, and stir in honey; cool a little, then pour over fruit, and sprinkle with desiccated coconut or toasted coconut strands. Serve chilled.

HEALTHY SWEETS

Here are two recipes which have been approved by my youngest daughter and her friends!

Fruity Squares
Makes 64
Calories: 35 a square

350g (12 oz) mixed dried
  fruit: dates, peaches,
  apricots, raisins
100g (4 oz) nuts: cashews,
  almonds, walnuts, hazels or
  brazils
100g (4 oz) desiccated coconut
  (unsweetened)

grated rind of 1 orange or
  lemon
a little orange juice
extra desiccated coconut for
  coating

Put dried fruit and nuts into a food processor and process until finely chopped. Then add coconut and grated rind and process again, adding enough orange juice to make a firm paste. Sprinkle a little desiccated coconut in a 20cm (8 inch) square tin, press fruit mixture on top, then sprinkle with more coconut and press down well. Put a weight on top and place in fridge to firm up. Then slice into 2cm (1 inch) squares.

Carob and Cashew Squares
Makes 21
Calories: 40 each

125g (4 oz) cashew nuts   ¼ vanilla pod (optional)
1 tablespoon carob powder   1 tablespoon thick honey

Put the cashew nuts, carob and vanilla pod, if used, into a liquidizer or food processor and whizz to a powder. Then add honey and process again to make a stiff paste. Put this into a 20×20cm (8×8 inch) shallow tin and press it out so that it is 1cm (½ inch) deep (it will only fill about a third of the tin). Put into the fridge to firm up, then make two cuts one way and 7 the other, to make 21 squares.

Wholemeal flour . . . help!

Once you start using wholefoods, you soon meet wholemeal*
flour – and at first you may wish you hadn't! In fact, it's got
a rather pleasant nutty flavour which soon makes white flour
seem very bland, but that's not the problem. The problem
comes when you start to try and actually bake with it.

Take wholemeal pastry, for instance. Instead of producing
a smooth, elastic, homogeneous mass that you can throw
around with thoughtless abandon, wholemeal pastry tends, at
the first attempt, to be very much a thing of shreds and patches.
This is mainly because wholemeal flour isn't as starchy as
white. I think the answer is to start with a half-and-half mixture

---

*Or wholewheat – the two terms are interchangeable, but not to be confused
 with wheatmeal which isn't the same.

of 85% and 100% wholemeal flour. (This is best also if the family aren't used to it and tend to be silly about trying new things.) As wholemeal pastry looks – well – browner than white, you might like to play up its wholesomeness by presenting your pie or tart in one of those thick, chunky handmade-type dishes, for a rather rustic meal.

Wholemeal flour makes a good fruit cake as well as, perhaps surprisingly, a good light sponge cake – and I enjoy serving this to my cynical friends who think wholemeal flour has to be stodgy.

But why bother to use wholemeal flour, anyway? Only that it still contains all the goodness which should be there, in the right proportions, including the fibre and the wheat germ. And the iron and calcium are all there naturally, instead of being added later in chemical form, as they are with white flour, along with preservatives, fungicides, anti-caking agents and goodness knows what other rubbish.

Wholemeal Pastry
Makes 200g (8 oz)
Calories: 1700 for whole quantity

200g (8 oz) wholemeal flour
100g (4 oz) unsalted butter, cut
  into pieces

3 tablespoons cold water

Sift the flour into a bowl, adding also the residue of bran which will be left behind in the sieve. Then rub in the butter with your fingertips. When the mixture looks like fine breadcrumbs, add the water and gently press mixture together to form a dough. Roll out in the usual way. I find it best to do this on a pastry board, then I simply slide the pastry off the board and into the tin or on to the pie or tart, thus avoiding breakages. Bake in the usual way in a hot oven, 200°–230°C (400°–450°F), gas mark 6–8.

If you want to increase the protein value of your pastry replace 40g (1½ oz) of the flour with that amount of soya flour. This makes 32 per cent more of the wheat protein available to you, since wheat and soya are complementary proteins.

Amazing Eggless, Sugarless, Fatless Cake

I was thrilled with this invention, which comes out just like a moist, rich fruit cake, yet contains none of the 'baddies'.
Makes one 900g (2 lb) loaf-size cake
Calories: 60 per 25g (1 oz)

225g (8 oz) cooking dates (not 'sugar-rolled')
275ml (10 fl oz) water
450g (1 lb) mixed dried fruit
175g (6 oz) plain wholewheat flour
1 tablespoon carob powder, optional

3 teaspoons baking powder
1 teaspoon mixed spice
grated rind of 1 orange or lemon
50g (2 oz) ground almonds
4 tablespoons orange juice
few flaked almonds for top

Set oven to 160°C (325°F), gas mark 3. Grease a 900g (2 lb) loaf tin and line with a strip of greaseproof or non-stick paper. Put dates and water into a saucepan and heat gently until dates are soft, then remove from heat and mash to break up dates. Add dried fruit, flour, carob powder, baking powder, spice, grated rind, ground almonds and orange juice. Spoon mixture into tin, level top. Sprinkle with almonds and bake for about 1½ hours, until a skewer inserted into centre comes out clean. Cool a little in tin, then turn cake out and finish cooling on a wire rack.

Unfired Christmas Cake

Here's another unusual one: a really 'alternative'-style Christmas cake that tastes delicious.
Makes one 450 (1 lb) loaf-size cake
Calories: 85 per 25g (1 oz)

225g (8 oz) chopped dates
225g (8 oz) brazils
225g (8 oz) rolled oats
125g (4 oz) mixed dried fruit
2 tablespoons honey
2 tablespoons carob powder
2 grated apples
grated rind of 2 oranges
2 tablespoons brandy or orange juice
50g (2 oz) ground almonds
2 teaspoons mixed spice

Line a 450g (1 lb) loaf tin with non-stick paper. If you've got a food processor, simply put everything into that and process until mixture holds together. Otherwise, heat the dates gently in a saucepan with a very little water until soft enough to mash, then transfer to a bowl. Chop or grind the brazil nuts and add to the date purée, together with the rest of the ingredients. Mix until well combined. Either way, press mixture into tin, put weight on top and leave in fridge for several hours. Turn out and serve in small slices; or coat with honey marzipan (below) and/or sugarless icing, page 103.

Honey Marzipan

Makes 250g (9 oz)
Calories: 1500 for whole amount

200g (7 oz) ground almonds
4 tablespoons clear honey
1 tablespoon lemon juice

Put all the ingredients into a bowl and mix gently together to form a firm dough.

Wholewheat Fruit Cake

In case the two cakes above are a bit too way-out for you, here's a more normal one which uses wholemeal flour.

Makes one 20cm (8 inch) round cake
Calories: 100 per 25g (1 oz)

225g (8 oz) wholemeal flour
2 teaspoons baking powder
½ teaspoon each of allspice, cinnamon and grated nutmeg
175g (6 oz) soft butter
125g (4 oz) raw muscovado sugar
3 free-range eggs, beaten

50g (2 oz) ground almonds
350g (12 oz) mixed raisins, sultanas and currants
50g (2 oz) dried apricots, washed and chopped
25g (1 oz) flaked almonds
grated rind of 1 orange
a little milk

Set oven to 160°C (325°F), gas mark 3. Grease and line a 20cm (8 inch) round tin. Sift flour, baking powder and spices on to a piece of greaseproof paper, adding the remaining bran which won't go through the sieve. Cream the butter and sugar until light and fluffy, then gradually beat in the egg, adding a little of the flour alternately if mixture shows signs of curdling. Then fold in remaining flour, dried fruit, flaked almonds, orange rind and enough milk (if necessary) to make a consistency which drops easily from the spoon. Spoon mixture into tin, level top. Bake for 1½–1¾ hours, until a skewer inserted in the middle comes out clean. Cool for 15 minutes in the tin, then turn out on to a wire rack. Strip off paper when cake has cooled.

Sponge Cake for Cynical Friends
Makes one 18cm (7 inch) sponge sandwich cake
Calories: 1200 for whole cake; filling extra, see below

125g (4 oz) wholemeal flour
4 free-range eggs
125g (4 oz) light muscovado
    sugar (not the very dark one,
    as it's too treacly for this)

for filling suggestions, see
below

Set oven to 190°C (375°F), gas mark 5. Grease two 18cm (7 inch) tins and line with a circle of greased greaseproof paper. Sift wholemeal flour on to a plate, adding the residue of bran from the sieve too. Whisk together eggs and sugar in an electric mixer, or with a hand whisk over a pan of boiling water, until thick and pale, and mixture leaves a trail on itself (about 5 minutes with the mixer, 15–20 minutes by hand). Fold in flour. Pour into the tins. Bake for about 10 minutes, until cakes have shrunk away from the edge of the tins and spring back when touched lightly. Cool on a wire rack that has been covered with a clean tea towel. When cool, sandwich with your choice of filling. Some ideas are:

the no-sugar icing on page 103 (950 calories for whole amount);
reduced-sugar or sugarless jam from the health shop (40–70 calories for 25g/1 oz, depending on type) or some fresh raspberries or strawberries (7 calories for 25g/1 oz), with or without a little whipped cream (100 calories for 25g/1 oz), whipped tofu, page 113 (180–200 calories for whole amount) or quark (30–45 calories for 25g/1 oz);
homemade sugarless conserve, page 116 (20 calories for 25g/ 1 oz);
honey mixed with almonds which have been powdered in the blender or an electric coffee mill (allow 80 calories for 25g/ 1 oz honey, 155 for 25g/1 oz almonds);
the date spread on page 116 (40 calories for 25g/1 oz);

101

a raw-sugar butter icing made by beating 50g (2 oz) unsalted butter and 50g (2 oz) light barbados sugar together until light (670 calories). A tablespoon of carob powder can be added to this (plus a little hot water) for a chocolaty flavour (720 calories).

Eggless Orange Sponge

You might think that a cake like this, made without eggs and with wholewheat flour, would be decidedly rock-like. I was afraid so too, but once I'd thought of the idea, I had to try it, and was amazed and delighted at the light, springy cake that resulted.

Makes one 20×30cm (8×12 inch) oblong, cutting into 14–16 pieces

Calories: 190–215 a piece

175g (6 oz) wholemeal flour
1 teaspoon baking powder
125g (4 oz) butter
125g (4 oz) light muscovado sugar

rind and juice of ½ orange
150ml (5 fl oz) milk
no-sugar icing (see below)

Set oven to 180°C (350°F), gas mark 4. Grease and line a 20×30cm (8×12 inch) swiss roll tin. Sift together the flour and baking powder, adding the residue of bran from the sieve too. Cream butter and sugar, then gently fold in sifted ingredients and orange rind alternately with the milk and orange juice. If the mixture looks a bit lumpy, beat it well and it will smooth out again. Spread in the prepared tin and bake for 25 minutes, until it springs back when touched. Cool in the tin, then pour over the icing. Cut into fingers when icing has set.

For chocolaty flavoured slices, leave out the orange and add 1 tablespoon carob powder and 3–4 tablespoons extra milk to the mixture. Cover with the carob version of the icing below.

No-Sugar Icing
Makes enough to coat 20×30cm (8×12 inch) oblong cake or top
of 18–20cm (7–8 inch) round cake
Calories: 950 for whole amount

125g (4 oz) coconut cream,
from health shops

2 tablespoons boiling water
a dash of honey or raw sugar

Grate the coconut cream, add boiling water and honey or sugar
and stir until creamy. Smooth cake with a knife dipped in
boiling water, and leave to set. Orange icing can be made with
the addition of a little grated orange rind;
For a chocolaty icing, stir in a teaspoonful of carob powder;
For lemon icing, use grated lemon rind.

Date Slices
Makes 14–16
Calories: 215–245 a piece

1½ times basic pastry recipe,
page 97

350g (12 oz) cooking dates
150ml (5 fl oz) water

Set oven to 180°C (350°F), gas mark 4. Grease a 20×30cm
(8×12 inch) swiss roll tin. Use half the pastry to line swiss roll
tin, roll out remainder to fit top. Break up dates and simmer
them in the water until they're soft, then cool. Spread date
mixture over the pastry in the tin, top with the remaining piece;
press down well and prick. Bake for 20 minutes. Cool in tin,
then cut into slices. This recipe makes use of the natural sugar
in the dates.

MAKING BREAD

Since about 30 per cent of our salt comes from the bread we eat, it's worth making your own low-salt loaves if you want to reduce your salt intake. You can leave out the salt altogether, or just use a little. If you make your own bread you also know exactly what goes into it! Here are two really easy recipes.

Quick Wholemeal Bread

In this loaf, the magic ingredient is the vitamin C which speeds up the rising process and means that a loaf can be ready in 1¾ hours.
Makes two 450g (1 lb) loaves
Calories: 70 for a 25g (1 oz) slice

700g (1½ lb) plain wholemeal
   flour
1 teaspoon salt
1 teaspoon raw sugar
15g (½ oz) butter

25g (1 oz) fresh yeast
400ml (¾ pint) tepid water
25mg ascorbic acid tablet,
   crushed, from chemists

Put flour, salt and sugar into a bowl and rub in the butter. Crumble the yeast into the water, add the ascorbic acid and stir until dissolved. Add yeast liquid to the flour and mix to a dough. Knead for 5 minutes, then cover with clingfilm and leave for 5 minutes. The dough will expand by one third.

Grease bread tins. Divide dough in half. Flatten each piece of dough out into a rectangle, then roll up lightly, pop roll into tin with seam-side down, then push the ends and sides of the loaf well down into the tin so that you get a nice rounded dome shape.

Pop the tins into a polythene carrier bag and leave until bread has doubled in size: 40–45 minutes at room temperature. Set oven so that it will have heated up to 230°C (450°F), gas mark 8, by the time the loaves have risen. Bake the bread for 30–35 minutes. Turn loaves out and cool on a wire rack.

Even Quicker Wholemeal Bread

This bread has a moist consistency and a springy texture; it's rather different from ordinary bread, but delicious in its own right. And it's a doddle to make!
Makes two 450g (1 lb) loaves
Calories: about 70 for a 25g (1 oz) slice

450g (1 lb) 100% wholemeal flour

50g (2 oz) kibbled wheat or medium oatmeal

1 dessertspoon clear honey or raw sugar

1 dessertspoon malt or molasses (optional)

1 teaspoon salt (optional)

25g (1 oz) fresh yeast

400ml (¾ pint) tepid water

extra kibbled wheat for topping

Put flour and wheat or oatmeal into a bowl with the honey or sugar and malt (or molasses) and salt (if using). Crumble the yeast into the water, stir until dissolved, then add to flour. Mix to a soft dough. Divide mixture between two greased 450g (1 lb) loaf tins. Sprinkle with kibbled wheat and cover with a piece of clingfilm. Set oven to 180°C (350°F), gas mark 4. Leave bread to stand at room temperature for about 30 minutes, until mixture has doubled in size. Remove clingfilm, bake loaves for about 30 minutes. Cool on wire rack.

Sugarless and Fatless Date and Walnut Loaf

This is 'fatless' in that it doesn't contain added fat, although there is of course some natural oil in the walnuts.

Beanfeast

Makes one 450g (1 lb) loaf, cutting into 10 slices
Calories: 150 a slice

175g (6 oz) dates
275ml (10 fl oz) water
175g (6 oz) plain wholewheat
   flour

3 teaspoons baking powder
75g (3 oz) walnuts, chopped
1 teaspoon vanilla

Put dates into a saucepan with the water and simmer gently until dates are reduced to a purée. Remove from heat and leave on one side to cool. Set oven to 180°C (350°F), gas mark 4. Line a 450g (1 lb) loaf tin with a strip of non-stick paper and grease. Sift flour and baking powder into a bowl, adding the residue of bran from the sieve too. Then add the walnuts, vanilla and cooled date mixture and stir well. Spoon into tin, bake for 50–60 minutes, until centre feels springy and a skewer inserted into the centre comes out clean. Cool on a wire rack. Serve cut into thick slices, and buttered if liked.

Easy Wholemeal Scones
Makes 12
Calories: 13 each

225g (8 oz) plain wholemeal
   flour
4 teaspoons baking powder
50g (2 oz) soft butter

50g (2 oz) raw barbados sugar
150ml (5 fl oz) skim milk

Set oven to 230°C (450°F), gas mark 8. Sift flour and baking powder into a bowl; add the bran left in the sieve too. Then rub in the butter, add the sugar and mix to a soft dough with the milk. Roll out 2cm (1 inch) thick and cut into rounds using a 5cm (2 inch) round cutter. Place on a floured baking sheet and bake for 12–15 minutes until risen. Cool on wire rack.

Home industries

The thing about wholefoods is that they grow on you. You start off going into your health shop to buy the odd bag of wholemeal flour or muesli base, and before you know where you are you're buying tiger nuts and tofu, making your own yoghurt and soya milk and sprouting your own beans. That's what happened to me, at any rate. So, in case you're the same, I've gathered together in this section all the recipes for homemade dairy produce (including non-milk varieties), preserves, ghee and beansprouts. Some of them, such as the soya milk, are fiddly but fun to make; others are very easy. And it's surprising how good they are.

Cottage Cheese
Calories: 45–50 per 25g (1 oz)
You can make cottage cheese at home and the finished product
has a splendid flavour, but you do need a lot of milk to make
quite a small quantity of cheese – 1 litre (2 pints) will make
about 225g (8 oz). If possible you really want to get untreated
milk (green top) for this, or goat's milk, then leave it outside
the fridge for several days until it goes sour. If you can't get
untreated milk, you can use ordinary pasteurized but you need
to add cultured buttermilk to sour it. Warm 1 litre (2 pints) of
milk until it's only just tepid (it should be a bit less than blood
heat) then stir in 2 teaspoons cultured buttermilk (which you
should be able to get at a large supermarket). Cover pan and
leave to stand in a warm room for about 24 hours. When it's
done, it will be solid underneath (but not lumpy like the bought
variety) with a thick crust on top, and when you cut it with a
knife you should see some clear whey coming out.

Put a piece of muslin or some layers of surgical gauze from
the chemist in a large metal sieve or colander set over a large
bowl, and pour through a kettleful of boiling water to sterilize
it. Then gently pour or ladle the soured milk into the cloth.
Leave for several hours for curds to settle, then gather up and
tie the cloth and suspend it above the bowl so that the remaining
whey can drip out. Leave overnight or for 8 hours or so. And
there's your cheese! You can use it as it is, with fruit; or add
a little salt and some fresh herbs for serving in a salad.

Yoghurt Cheese
Calories: 45–50 per 25g (1 oz)
This is simpler than the above, and tastes marvellous. All you
do is put a piece of muslin or some gauze over a metal sieve,
scald by pouring through some boiling water, then put your
yoghurt into the muslin and leave for 5–8 hours. Next, gather

up the muslin, tie, and hang over the bowl to drip for another 8 hours or so. Your cheese is then ready and is delicious with fruit or salads.

Yoghurt

Calories: 15–20 per 25g (1 oz)

Making yoghurt is like making bread: it's easy when you do it often. The first batch is always a bit hit-and-miss and the batches improve as you go along. So I think it's worth making fairly small batches frequently. The best milk to use (from the health point of view) is goat's milk, which some health shops and big supermarkets sell; otherwise use fresh skim milk. If you want a thick yoghurt you need to reduce the milk by half by gentle boiling (with an upturned saucer or glass 'milk saver' in the base to prevent it boiling over), or you can simply add some powdered goat's milk (obtainable but expensive) or skim milk to achieve the same effect.

To make the yoghurt, scald 575ml (1 pint), then let it cool to blood heat. Whisk in your milk powder if you're using this, together with 1 tablespoon of live yoghurt. Make sure it is 'live' – most of the stuff sold in supermarkets now isn't. Mix well. Scald a thermos flask or bowl with boiling water to sterilize and warm it, then pour in your yoghurt mixture. Wrap the bowl in a warm towel, cover it and leave it in a warm place such as an airing cupboard or corner by a radiator. Or use Doris Grant's method which she describes in *Your Daily Food*: fit small glass jars snugly into a polystyrene bulb bowl and cover with an expanded polystyrene tile (the sort you put on bathroom ceilings for insulation). Whichever method you use, leave the yoghurt undisturbed for 5–8 hours until it's firm. It will firm up even more in the fridge.

Vegan Yoghurt
Makes 575ml (1 pint)
Calories: 15 per 25g (1 oz)

575ml (1 pint) soya milk
yoghurt starter culture, from
   health shops

Any yoghurt culture will work as well on soya milk as it does
on dairy milk. Put the soya milk into a saucepan and bring to
the boil, then cool to lukewarm. Add the starter as directed on
the packet, stir well. Pour the mixture into a thermos flask or
large jar or bowl which has been sterilized by being rinsed out
with boiling water. Cover the jar or bowl with clingfilm or foil
and wrap in a warm towel. Leave in a warm place for 5–8 hours,
until set, then chill in the fridge. This first batch will not be 100
per cent vegan, but a tablespoonful of this can be used to start
the next batch, which will be. The yoghurt gets thicker and
better each time.

Soya Milk   Super Version
This is the most delicious milk, far nicer than dairy milk! It's
a fiddle to make, but rewarding when you see the beautiful
white liquid. It works out at about a third of the price of bought
soya milk.
Makes about 1.2 litres (2 pints)
Calories: 15 per 30ml (1 fl oz), approximately

225g (8 oz) soya beans   dash of honey or raw sugar
1 vanilla pod
1 tablespoon cold-pressed
   sunflower oil

Soak the beans in plenty of water for 2 days, changing the water twice a day. Liquidize beans with 1.5 litres (2½ pints) water. Pour mixture through a sieve lined with a piece of muslin, squeezing through as much liquid as possible into a large saucepan. Add the vanilla pod. Heat liquid to boiling point, then remove vanilla pod and liquidize again with the oil, and a dash of honey or sugar to taste. Strain through muslin again. (The vanilla pod can be washed, dried and used a number of times. Alternatively, you can use half a vanilla pod only and liquidize it with the milk for a strong and very delicious flavour. But since vanilla pods don't come cheap, this does put up the price of the soya-pinta.)

Soya Milk   Quick and Easy Version

This isn't nearly as delicate as the soya milk above, but is useful for cooking.
Makes 1.2 litres (2 pints)
Calories: 15 per 30 ml (1 fl oz), approximately

75g (3 oz) flour	1 tablespoon cold-pressed oil
1.2 litres (2 pints) water	dash of honey or raw sugar

Whisk or liquidize together. The protein in soya milk is quite similar to ordinary milk, so near enough the same complementary effects should apply if substituted for milk in recipes.

Tiger Nut Milk

Tiger nuts (sometimes called chufa nuts) are little chewy brown rhizomes which you can sometimes get from the health shop. They're quite pricey, but make a wonderful milk for a special treat and it still works out cheaper (by about 25 per cent) than bought soya milk. It's also much easier to make than soya milk.

111

Makes 1.2 litres (2 pints)
Calories: 15 per 30ml (1 fl oz), approximately

250g (8 oz) tiger nuts   1.2 litres (2 pints) water

Wash the chufa nuts, then liquidize them with the water. Leave to stand 3–4 hours, then strain and use as milk. (The strained-off pulp can be eaten with muesli or incorporated into nut cutlets if you want to be really thrifty.) This milk is delicious chilled as a drink (I like the flavour much better than cow's milk) or poured over cereal, fruit or puddings.

Tofu

I've adapted this recipe – which makes quite a firm-textured tofu – from *Vegan Cooking*, by Leah Leneman, published by Thorsons. Nigari gives the best results and can be bought from health shops.
Makes approx. 100g (4 oz)
Calories: 15 per 25g (1 oz)

575ml (1 pint) soya milk, made   4 tablespoons hot water
  as above
½ teaspoon Nigari or Epsom
  salts

Put soya milk into a pan and bring to the boil. Dissolve the Nigari or Epsom salts in the hot water and add to the milk. Leave for 5 minutes for mixture to curdle. Line a sieve with a piece of muslin. Pour curdled mixture through, separating curds from liquid (liquid will not be needed). Fold muslin over to cover curds and place weight on top. Leave for 1 hour. Remove curds – the tofu – from muslin and store in a bowl of cold water in the fridge.

Nut Cream

This is delicious, and much healthier than dairy cream.
Makes about 250ml (8 fl oz)
Calories: 760 for full amount

125g (4 oz) cashew nuts or
  blanched almonds
150ml (5 fl oz) water

dash of honey or raw sugar
real vanilla extract or a piece of
  vanilla pod

Simply put everything into a liquidizer or food processor and whizz to a cream. If you're using the vanilla pod, your cream will have some black specks in it, but will taste superb. (Any larger pieces of vanilla pod which don't get broken down by the blender can be removed and used again.) If you want a thinner cream, simply add more water.

Tofu 'Whipped' Cream

For this you need firm tofu – homemade or bought from a health shop or Chinese shop. You could use the vacuum-packed tofu which you can buy, but that will not give such a thick effect.
Makes 225g (8 oz)
Calories: 180–200 for whole amount

225g (8 oz) tofu
2 teaspoons honey or raw
  sugar

real vanilla extract or a piece of
  vanilla pod

Drain water from tofu. Break tofu into rough pieces and place in blender or food processor with the honey or sugar and the vanilla extract or pod and whizz to a thick cream. As with the nut cream above, using a vanilla pod will result in a wonderful flavour but slightly speckled appearance. This is also delicious flavoured with some triple distilled rose water or orange flower water (Langdales) or some grated orange or lemon rind.

Hard Soya Cheese

I'm grateful to the Vegan Society for permission to use this recipe which makes a useful substitute for hard cheese if you don't eat dairy produce.
Makes 225g (8 oz)
Calories: 160 per 25g (1 oz)

125g (4 oz) Tomor margarine or Nutter white vegetable fat, both from health shops

1 teaspoon yeast extract
125g (4 oz) soya flour

Put the fat and yeast extract into a saucepan and heat gently until melted. Remove from the heat and stir in the soya flour; mix well. Pour into a mould or bowl to set. The result will be a hard cheese that you can slice or grate, and even toast under the grill. Soya cheese and wholewheat bread are complementary proteins, like ordinary cheese with bread.

Fermented Nut Cheese

This can best be described as a nutty version of cottage cheese, but it's a delicious product in its own right. It's also very good for you, because, like real live yoghurt, it contains lactic acid which encourages your gut to produce helpful bacteria which then get rid of the bad ones. (Meat, by the way, does exactly the opposite; it encourages the baddies.)
Makes 300g (10 oz)
Calories: 1100 for whole quantity

50g (2 oz) blanched almonds
75g (3 oz) walnuts
50g (2 oz) sunflower seeds
100ml (4 fl oz) water

seasonings as required: fresh
chopped herbs, a little
tahini

Grind the nuts and sunflower seeds finely, add the water and mix well. Stir in the herbs and tahini, if used. Place in a bowl covered with a tea towel and leave to ferment for about 8–12 hours in a warm place.

Peanut Butter
Makes 225g (8 oz)
Calories: 180 per 25g (1 oz)

225g (8 oz) shelled raw
  peanuts

cold-pressed vegetable oil,
preferably ground nut

Spread the nuts out on a baking sheet and let them roast gently at the bottom of the oven while it's on for something else. They're done when the skins rub off, revealing a golden brown nut underneath. Grind as finely as possible in a blender, electric coffee grinder or food processor. Then put into a bowl and beat in enough oil to make a spreading consistency. (I find this method better than adding oil to the nuts in the blender, which usually results in a sticky mess when I do it.) Homemade peanut butter, as well as being cheaper, avoids the additives which are slipped into most commercial peanut butters (including sugar, would you believe!). Keep the peanut butter in the fridge. The oil will separate, but this just proves you've got a really natural product without stabilizers and emulsifiers. Simply give the peanut butter a stir before you use it.

When using any nuts it's important to make sure they're fresh; with peanuts it's specially important to check there are no signs of mould, which is poisonous. This shouldn't be a problem if you buy small quantities of fresh peanuts from a reputable shop, store them in a tin or jar in a dry place, and use them up fairly quickly.

Sugarless Apricot Conserve

This is simple to make and tastes wonderful. It makes an excellent healthy substitute for either jam or marmalade, but it doesn't keep in the same way, so make it in small quantities.
Makes about 225g (8 oz)
Calories: 20 per 25g (1 oz)

125g (4 oz) dried apricots – the unsulphured ones from health shops are best

250ml (½ pint) water
grated rind and juice of 1 small well-scrubbed orange

Soak the apricots in the water overnight. Next day put them into a saucepan with their soaking water and the orange juice and rind. Bring to the boil then simmer gently, with a lid on the pan, for 40–45 minutes, until the mixture is thick, soft and jam-like. Stir mixture occasionally and add a little extra water if necessary to prevent sticking. Cool, then transfer to a jar and store in the fridge.

Yummy Date Spread

This is popular with the children, and the carob version is a good healthy substitute for chocolate spread.
Makes about 225g (8 oz)
Calories: 40 per 25g (1 oz)

225g (8 oz) dates

orange or apple juice

If you have a food processor, you can simply put the dates into that, with enough juice to make a soft, spreadable mixture. Alternatively, put the dates into a saucepan with 150ml (5 fl oz) water and heat gently until dates are soft. Then mash to a purée.

For the 'chocolate spread' variation, simply stir in a tablespoonful of carob powder and a few drops of real vanilla extract (or add a piece of vanilla pod to the dates when you whizz them in the food processor).

Another variation is to add a few almonds: whizz these up in the food processor with the dates, or powder them in a liquidizer or electric coffee grinder, before adding them.

Fresh Fruit 'Jam'

In the summer, when fresh soft fruits are at their peak, you can make a wonderful raw 'jam' by simply mashing raspberries, strawberries or redcurrants with a little clear honey. Delicious on homemade wholewheat bread (you don't even need butter). Or try it on homemade wholewheat scones with a dollop of quark, homemade soft cheese or thick natural yoghurt for a marvellous and healthy cream tea!

Sugarless Chutney

Makes approx. 350g (12 oz)
Calories: 50 per 25g (1 oz)

125g (4 oz) dates
125g (4 oz) sultanas
1 small onion, finely chopped

1 teaspoon pickling spice
6 tablespoons cider vinegar or
  wine vinegar

Chop the dates roughly, then put into a pan (not an aluminium one) with the rest of the ingredients. Bring to the boil, then heat gently for about 15 minutes, stirring occasionally, until the onion is tender. Keep in a container in the fridge. The chutney can be thinned, if necessary, by adding a little water, apple juice or extra vinegar.

HOW TO SPROUT BEANS, GRAINS AND LENTILS

Sprouted beans, grains and lentils are highly nutritious, being rich in vitamins and minerals and containing high-quality protein. As I said in the Introduction, it takes 20 lb of vegetable protein to produce 1 lb of animal protein; but when you sprout seeds you have a protein factory the right way round – increasing the original food value (by up to 600 per cent!).

Sprouting is easy to do. All you need is a jar (a big coffee jar is ideal), a piece of muslin or J cloth to go over the top, secured with an elastic band, and some beans or seeds. Most types are suitable, with the exception of red kidney beans (and I personally would not do large beans such as butter beans). Choose, for instance, from chickpeas, alfalfa seeds, continental lentils, sunflower seeds, mung beans, aduki beans and whole wheat grains. Put half a cupful of chosen beans, grains or lentils into your jar, cover with cold water and leave to soak for 8–12 hours. Put your piece of muslin or J cloth over the top of the jar. Then drain off the water, fill the jar with fresh water, swish it round and then pour it all out again. All this can be done without removing the muslin or J cloth which prevents the seeds or beans falling out and blocking the sink. This rinsing has to be repeated twice a day, to keep the seeds damp (but they must on no account be left soaking in water or they'll rot rather than sprout!). I keep my seeds by the sink to remind me about the rinsing. It's really quite satisfying to see the sprouts developing day by day and in 2–4 days they're ready to use. They can be used straight away, to add crunch and nourishment to salads and sandwiches, or they'll keep in the fridge for several days.

If you want to make long juicy beansprouts like the ones you can buy, you need to use a slightly different method. Use the little green mung beans and soak them overnight in water as usual. Then put them into a large colander or plastic draining bowl (lined with a piece of kitchen paper to prevent them falling through). Spread them out well, then put a piece of polythene and a heavy weight (like a 3 lb bag of flour) on top. Twice a day remove these and rinse the beans as usual.

You can also use this colander method (without the weight and polythene) for all the other seeds and beans if you find it more convenient. If you get really addicted, or if you're cooking for lots of people, you might even like to invest in a gardener's large round plastic sieve, which I have found to be ideal, when lined with kitchen paper! On a smaller scale, you can buy (from many health shops) a special sprouter which consists of three sprouting trays (that means it's easy to have three lots of sprouts on the go at the same time!), with a water-collecting bowl underneath (which saves the rinsing routine).

Ghee
Makes about 300ml (11 fl oz)
Calories: 125 per tablespoonful

225g (8 oz) unsalted butter

Cut the butter into pieces, put into a heavy-based saucepan and heat gently until butter has melted. Don't let it brown. When it has melted, give it a stir, then let it simmer, without a lid on the pan, over a very low heat, for about 45 minutes, or until the solids at the bottom of the melted butter turn golden brown, and the butter on top turns transparent. Strain the ghee through a sieve lined with four layers of damp muslin or gauze. If any of the solids come through, strain the ghee again; it must be perfectly clear otherwise it won't keep properly. Best stored in the fridge.

The trouble is,
it's all so fattening...

Fashions in slimming diets change. When I wrote the first edition of *Beanfeast* in 1974, such things as rice, bread, lentils and pasta were the arch-enemies of slimmers, who were urged to eat plenty of protein. People about to embark on wholefood eating genuinely worried about the effects this would have on their waistline. Now things have changed, and wholewheat bread, pasta and potatoes are all the slimming-rage!

For most people, the best slimming plan is simply a modified, calorie-counted version of a normal day's eating. Here is an example, based on wholefood principles and allowing for 1200–1400 calories a day, which for most people gives a steady weight-loss of around 1½–2 lb a week.

Normal Meals	Slimmer's Version	
	300ml (½ pint) skim milk allowed for day	100
BREAKFAST		
muesli base, soaked over-	25g (1 oz) muesli base	100
night with sunflower seeds,	15g (½ oz) sunflower seeds	85
raisins and sliced banana,	15g (½ oz) raisins	35
topped with skim milk;	1 medium banana	80
	skim milk from allowance	
		300
OR		
wholewheat toast with a little	2 pieces, scraping butter	200
butter and marmalade;	25g (1 oz) marmalade	75
		275
OR		
natural low-fat yoghurt	150g (5 oz) natural yoghurt	75
with chopped banana;	1 medium	80
sprinkling of wheat germ	1 tablespoon	25
		180
LUNCH		
large salad with oil and	450g (1 lb) any vegetables	
vinegar dressing;	except potatoes, sweetcorn	
	or avocado	64
	1 tablespoon of dressing	35
wholewheat bread or baked	50g (2 oz) bread or 125 g (4 oz)	
potato and butter;	potato	150
	15g (½ oz) butter	111
grated cheese or cottage	25g (1 oz) hard cheese or	
cheese;	125g (4 oz) cottage cheese	120
fresh fruit	1 apple, orange or pear	50
		530

Beanfeast

MAIN MEAL		
main dish from this book;	any dish up to 300 calories	300
lightly cooked vegetables or salad;	up to 350g (12 oz) vegetables (not potato, avocado or sweetcorn)	48
pudding as required	fresh fruit as for lunch, or pudding if calories allow	50
		400

EXTRAS		
fresh fruit, dried fruit and nuts, wholewheat bread	fresh fruit, carrot or celery sticks, sprigs, of raw cauliflower	
	TOTAL	1330

After about four weeks you may find that your weight sticks; if so, knock off 100 calories, and do the same if the weight sticks again. But don't go lower than 1200. You'll lose weight steadily this way – 1½–2 lb a week. There's no point in trying to lose weight any quicker than this, because the maximum amount of actual fat you can lose in a week is 2 lb; more than that, and it's muscle (or excess water), so it's pointless to be too strict. You might as well allow yourself a fairly high calorie ration, as above, and enjoy your food while you're slimming! Once you've reached your ideal weight, you can either increase your calorie intake methodically by 100 calories each week until your weight stabilizes, or you can just be freer about sizes of portions and little extras.

Index

Index

Index

Index

Index

Rose Elliot Horoscopes

In addition to writing cookery books, Rose Elliot also practises astrology. Her character readings have proved so popular that Rose and her husband are now using a computer to make them available to a wider public.

If you would like to see what Rose has to say about your character, and how you can make the most of your gifts, send your name, date, time and place of birth, with £10 or £13 ($25) overseas to:

Rose Elliot Horoscopes
The Old Rectory
Bishopstoke
Eastleigh
Hampshire SO5 6BH

Or write to the above address for further details and an application form.